The absolute unlawfulness of the stage-entertainment fully demonstrated. By William Law, A.M. The second edition.

William Law

ECCO
PRINT EDITIONS

Eighteenth Century
Collections Online
Print Editions

Gale ECCO Print Editions

Relive history with *Eighteenth Century Collections Online*, now available in print for the independent historian and collector. This series includes the most significant English-language and foreign-language works printed in Great Britain during the eighteenth century, and is organized in seven different subject areas including literature and language; medicine, science, and technology; and religion and philosophy. The collection also includes thousands of important works from the Americas.

The eighteenth century has been called "The Age of Enlightenment." It was a period of rapid advance in print culture and publishing, in world exploration, and in the rapid growth of science and technology – all of which had a profound impact on the political and cultural landscape. At the end of the century the American Revolution, French Revolution and Industrial Revolution, perhaps three of the most significant events in modern history, set in motion developments that eventually dominated world political, economic, and social life.

In a groundbreaking effort, Gale initiated a revolution of its own: digitization of epic proportions to preserve these invaluable works in the largest online archive of its kind. Contributions from major world libraries constitute over 175,000 original printed works. Scanned images of the actual pages, rather than transcriptions, recreate the works *as they first appeared.*

Now for the first time, these high-quality digital scans of original works are available via print-on-demand, making them readily accessible to libraries, students, independent scholars, and readers of all ages.

For our initial release we have created seven robust collections to form one the world's most comprehensive catalogs of 18th century works.

Initial Gale ECCO Print Editions collections include:

History and Geography

Rich in titles on English life and social history, this collection spans the world as it was known to eighteenth-century historians and explorers. Titles include a wealth of travel accounts and diaries, histories of nations from throughout the world, and maps and charts of a world that was still being discovered. Students of the War of American Independence will find fascinating accounts from the British side of conflict.

Social Science

Delve into what it was like to live during the eighteenth century by reading the first-hand accounts of everyday people, including city dwellers and farmers, businessmen and bankers, artisans and merchants, artists and their patrons, politicians and their constituents. Original texts make the American, French, and Industrial revolutions vividly contemporary.

Medicine, Science and Technology

Medical theory and practice of the 1700s developed rapidly, as is evidenced by the extensive collection, which includes descriptions of diseases, their conditions, and treatments. Books on science and technology, agriculture, military technology, natural philosophy, even cookbooks, are all contained here.

Literature and Language

Western literary study flows out of eighteenth-century works by Alexander Pope, Daniel Defoe, Henry Fielding, Frances Burney, Denis Diderot, Johann Gottfried Herder, Johann Wolfgang von Goethe, and others. Experience the birth of the modern novel, or compare the development of language using dictionaries and grammar discourses.

Religion and Philosophy

The Age of Enlightenment profoundly enriched religious and philosophical understanding and continues to influence present-day thinking. Works collected here include masterpieces by David Hume, Immanuel Kant, and Jean-Jacques Rousseau, as well as religious sermons and moral debates on the issues of the day, such as the slave trade. The Age of Reason saw conflict between Protestantism and Catholicism transformed into one between faith and logic -- a debate that continues in the twenty-first century.

Law and Reference

This collection reveals the history of English common law and Empire law in a vastly changing world of British expansion. Dominating the legal field is the *Commentaries of the Law of England* by Sir William Blackstone, which first appeared in 1765. Reference works such as almanacs and catalogues continue to educate us by revealing the day-to-day workings of society.

Fine Arts

The eighteenth-century fascination with Greek and Roman antiquity followed the systematic excavation of the ruins at Pompeii and Herculaneum in southern Italy; and after 1750 a neoclassical style dominated all artistic fields. The titles here trace developments in mostly English-language works on painting, sculpture, architecture, music, theater, and other disciplines. Instructional works on musical instruments, catalogs of art objects, comic operas, and more are also included.

The BiblioLife Network

This project was made possible in part by the BiblioLife Network (BLN), a project aimed at addressing some of the huge challenges facing book preservationists around the world. The BLN includes libraries, library networks, archives, subject matter experts, online communities and library service providers. We believe every book ever published should be available as a high-quality print reproduction; printed on-demand anywhere in the world. This insures the ongoing accessibility of the content and helps generate sustainable revenue for the libraries and organizations that work to preserve these important materials.

The following book is in the "public domain" and represents an authentic reproduction of the text as printed by the original publisher. While we have attempted to accurately maintain the integrity of the original work, there are sometimes problems with the original work or the micro-film from which the books were digitized. This can result in minor errors in reproduction. Possible imperfections include missing and blurred pages, poor pictures, markings and other reproduction issues beyond our control. Because this work is culturally important, we have made it available as part of our commitment to protecting, preserving, and promoting the world's literature.

GUIDE TO FOLD-OUTS MAPS and OVERSIZED IMAGES

The book you are reading was digitized from microfilm captured over the past thirty to forty years. Years after the creation of the original microfilm, the book was converted to digital files and made available in an online database.

In an online database, page images do not need to conform to the size restrictions found in a printed book. When converting these images back into a printed bound book, the page sizes are standardized in ways that maintain the detail of the original. For large images, such as fold-out maps, the original page image is split into two or more pages

Guidelines used to determine how to split the page image follows:

• Some images are split vertically; large images require vertical and horizontal splits.
• For horizontal splits, the content is split left to right.
• For vertical splits, the content is split from top to bottom.
• For both vertical and horizontal splits, the image is processed from top left to bottom right.

THE ABSOLUTE

UNLAWFULNESS

OF THE

Stage-Entertainment

FULLY Demonstrated.

By *WILLIAM LAW*, A.M.

The SECOND EDITION.

LONDON:

Printed for W. and J. INNYS, at the *West-*
End of St. *Paul's.* MDCCXXVI.

(Price Six-Pence.)

THE
Absolute Unlawfulness
OF THE
STAGE-*Entertainment.*

 Am sensible that the Title of this little-Book will, to the Generality of People, seem too high a Flight, that it will be look'd upon as the Effect of a Fanatical Spirit, carrying Matters higher than the Sobriety of Religion requireth I have only one Thing to ask of such People, that they will suspend their Judgment for a while, and be content to read so small a Treatise as this is, before they pass any judgment either upon the Merits of the Subject, or the Temper of the Writer.

Had a Person, some Years ago, in the Times of *Popery,* wrote against the *Worship* of *Images,* as a Worship absolutely unlawful; our Ancestors would have look'd upon him as a Man of a very *irregular* Spirit Now it is possible for the present Age to be as much mistaken in their *Pleasures,* as the

A 2 former

former were in their *Devotions*, and that the allow'd Diverfions of thefe Times may be as great a Contradiction to the
moft Effential Doctrines of Chriftianity, as the *Superftitions*
and *Corruptions* of the former Ages. All therefore that I defire, is only a little *Free-thinking* upon this Subject; and that
People will not as blindly reject all Reafon, when it examines
their Pleafures, as fome blindly reject all Reafon, when it
examines the Nature of their Devotions

It is poffible that *fomething* that is called a *Diverfion*, may
be as contrary to the whole Nature of Religion, as any invented Superftition, and perhaps more dangerous to thofe that
comply with it As the Worfhip of *Images* was a great Sin,
tho' under a Pretence of Piety, fo the Entertainment of the
Stage may be very finful, tho' it is only intended as a Diverfion

For if the Worfhip of Images did not ceafe to be finful,
tho' it was intended for pious Purpofes, it muft be great
Weaknefs to imagine, that the Entertainment of the *Stage*
cannot be any great Sin, becaufe it is only ufed as a Diverfion

Yet this is a Way of reafoning that a great many People
fall into They fay, Diverfions are lawful, that the *Stage* is
only a Diverfion, that People go to it without meaning any
Harm, and therefore there can be no Sin in it

But if thefe People were to hear a Man fay, that Religion
is lawful, that the Worfhip of Images was an Act of Religion, that he us'd Images as a Means of Religious Devotion,
and therefore there could be no Sin in it . they would migh-
tily lament the Bigotry and Blindnefs of his Mind Yet furely this is as wife and reafonable, as for a Perfon to fay, I go
to a Play, only as to a Diverfion I mean no Harm, and
therefore there can be no Sin in it For if Practices may be
exceeding finful, tho' they are intended for pious Ends, certainly Practices may be very abominable, tho' they are only
ufed as Diverfions

When therefore we condemn the *Blindnefs* of fome Chriftian Countries, for conforming to fuch grofs Corruptions of
Religion, we fhould do well to remember, that they have
thus much to be pleaded in their Excufe, that what they do,
is under a Notion of Piety, that it is in obedience to the
Authority both of Church and State, and that they are at
the fame time kept entire Strangers to the Scriptures But
how juftly may the fame Blindnefs be charged upon us, if it
fhould appear, that without having any of their Excufes, our

Pub-

Publick, Stated Diverſions are as contrary to Scripture, and the fundamental Doctrines of Religion, as any of the groſſeſt Inſtances of Superſtition? If we hold it lawful to go to wicked, ſinful Diverſions; we are as great Strangers to True Religion, as they who are pleas'd with buying *Indulgences*, and worſhip Pieces of holy Wood

For, a *Sinful Diverſion* is the ſame Abſurdity in Religion, as a *Corrupt Worſhip*, and it ſhews the ſame Blindneſs of Mind, and Corruption of Heart, whether we ſin againſt God in the *Church*, or in our *Cloſets*, or in the *Play-Houſe* If there is any thing contrary to Religion in any of theſe Places, it brings us under the ſame Guilt There may, perhaps, be this difference, that God may be leſs diſpleaſed with ſuch Corruptions as we comply with thro' a blind Devotion, than with ſuch as we indulge our ſelves in thro' a Wantonneſs of Mind, and a Fondneſs for Diverſions

The Matter therefore ſtands thus If it ſhould appear that the Stage-Entertainment is entirely ſinful, that it is contrary to more Doctrines of Scripture, than the Worſhip of *Images*; then it follows, that all who defend it, and take their Share of it, are in the ſame State, as they who worſhip *Images*, and defend Drunkenneſs and Intemperance For, to defend, or ſupport any ſinful Diverſion, is the ſame thing as Supporting or Defending any other ſinful Practice It therefore as much concerns us to know, whether our Diverſions are reaſonable, and conformable to Religion, as to know, whether our Religion be reaſonable, and conformable to Truth For, if we allow our ſelves in Diverſions that are contrary to Religion, we are in no better a State than thoſe, whoſe Religion is contrary to Truth

I have mentioned the Worſhip of *Images*, becauſe it is ſo great a Corruption in Religion, ſo contrary to Scripture, and ſo juſtly abhorr'd by all the Reform'd Churches, that the Reader may hence learn what he is to think of himſelf, if the *Stage* is ever his Diverſion For I am fully perſuaded, that he will here find Arguments againſt the *Stage*, as ſtrong and plain as any that can be urg'd againſt the Worſhip of *Images*, or any other Corruption of the moſt corrupt Religion

Let it therefore be obſerv'd, that the Stage is not here condemn'd, as ſome other Diverſions, becauſe they are dangerous, and likely to be Occaſions of Sin, but that it is condemn'd, as Drunkenneſs and ewdneſs, as Lying and Prophaneneſs are to be condem. not as Things that may only

ly

ly be the Occasions of Sin, but as such as are in their own Nature grossly sinful.

You go to hear a *Play* I tell you, that you go to hear *Ribaldry* and *Prophaneness* ; that you entertain your Mind with extravagant Thoughts, wild *Rant*, *blasphemous Speeches*, *wanton Amours*, *prophane Jests*, and *impure Passions*. If you ask me, where is the Sin of all this? You may as well ask me, where is the Sin of *Swearing* and *Lying* For it is not only a Sin against this or that particular Text of Scripture, but it is a Sin against the *whole Nature* and Spirit of our Religion

It is a Contradiction to all Christian Holiness, and to all the Methods of arriving at it For, can any one think that he has a true Christian Spirit, that his Heart is changed as it ought to be, that he is born again of God, whilst he is diverting himself with the Lewdness, Impudence, Prophaneness, and impure Discourses of the Stage? Can he think that he is endeavouring to be holy as Christ is holy, to live by his Wisdom, and be full of his Spirit, so long as he allows himself in such an Entertainment? For there is nothing in the Nature of Christian Holiness, but what is all contrary to the whole Spirit and Temper of this Entertainment. That Disposition of Heart, which is to take pleasure in the various Representations of the *Stage*, is as directly contrary to that Disposition of Heart which Christianity requireth, as Revenge is contrary to Meekness, or Malice to Good-will Now that which is thus contrary to the whole Nature and Spirit of Religion, is certainly much more condemned, than that which is only contrary to some particular Part of it

But this is plainly the Case of the *Stage* It is an Entertainment that consists of lewd, impudent, prophane Discourses, and, as such, is contrary to the *whole Nature* of our Religion. For, all the Parts of Religion, its whole Nature, has only this one Design, To give us Purity of Heart, to change the Temper and Taste of our Souls, and fill us with such holy Tempers, as may make us fit to live with God in the Society of pure and glorious Spirits

An Entertainment therefore which applies to the Corruption of our Nature, which awakens our disorder'd Passions, and teaches to relish Lewdness, immoral Rant, and Prophaneness, is exceeding sinful, not only as it is a Breach of some particular Duty, but as it contradicts the *whole Nature*, and opposes *every Part* of our Religion.

For

For this Diversion, which confists of such Difcourfes as thefe, injures us in a very different manner from other Sins. For, as Difcourfes are an Application to our whole Soul, as they entertain the Heart, and awaken and employ all our Paffions, fo they more fatally undo all that Religion has done, than feveral other Sins. For, as Religion confifts in a right Turn of Mind, as it is a State of the Heart, fo whatever fupports a quite contrary Turn of Mind, and State of Heart, has all the Contrariety to Religion that it can poffibly have.

St *John* faith, *Hereby we know that he abideth in us, by the Spirit which he hath given us.* There is no other certain Sign of our belonging to Chrift. Every other Sign may deceive us· All the External Parts of Religion may be in vain; it is only a State of our Mind and Spirit, that is a certain Proof that we are in a true State of Chriftianity. And the Reafon is plain, becaufe Religion has no other End, than to alter our Spirit, and give us new Difpofitions of Heart, fuitable to its Purity and Holinefs. That therefore which immediately applies to our Spirit, which fupports a wrong Turn of Mind, which betrays our Hearts into impure Delights, deftroys all our Religion, becaufe it deftroys that Turn of Mind and Spirit, which is the fole End and Defign of all our Religion.

When therefore you are asked why it is unlawful to fwear; you can anfwer, becaufe it is contrary to the Third Commandment. But if you are asked, why it is unlawful to ufe the Entertainment of the Stage, you can carry your Anfwer farther; becaufe it is an Entertainment that is contrary to all the Parts, the whole Nature of Religion, and contradicts every holy Temper, which the Spirit of Chriftianity requireth. So that if you live in the ufe of this Diverfion, you have no Grounds to hope, that you have the Spirit and Heart of a Chriftian.

Thus ftands the firft Argument againft the *Stage*. It has all the Weight in it, that the whole Weight of Religion can give to any Argument.

If you are only for the Form of Religion, you may take the Diverfion of the Stage along with it, but if you defire the *Spirit* of Religion, if you defire to be truly religious in Heart and Mind, it is as neceffary to renounce and abhor the Stage, as to feek to God, and pray for the Guidance of his Holy Spirit.

Secondly,

Secondly, Let the next Argument againſt the *Stage* be ta-ken from its manifeſt Contrariety to this important Paſſage of Scripture *Let no corrupt communication proceed out of your mouth, but that which is good to the uſe of edifying, that it may miniſter grace to the hearers And grieve not the holy Spirit of God, whereby ye are ſealed to the day of redemption.*

Here we ſee, that all corrupt and unedifying Communica-tion is abſolutely ſinful, and forbidden in Scripture for this Reaſon, becauſe it *grieves the Holy Ghoſt,* and ſeparates *Him* from us. But if it be thus unlawful to have any corrupt Communication of our own, can we think it lawful to go to Places ſet apart for that Purpoſe? To give our Money, and hire Perſons to corrupt our Hearts with ill Diſcourſes, and inflame all the diſorderly Paſſions of our Nature! We have the Authority of Scripture to affirm, that *evil Communication corrupts good Manners,* and that *unedifying Diſcourſes grieve the Holy Spirit*

Now the *Third* Commandment is not more plain and ex-preſs againſt *Swearing,* than this Doctrine is plain and poſi-tive againſt going to the *Play-Houſe* If you ſhould ſee a Perſon that acknowledges the *Third* Commandment to be a divine Prohibition againſt Swearing; yet going to a *Houſe,* and giving his *Money* to Perſons, who were there met to *Curſe* and *Swear* in fine Language, and invent *Muſical Oaths and Imprecations,* would you not think him mad in the high-eſt degree ? Now conſider whether there be a leſs degree of Madneſs in going to the Play-Houſe You own that God has called you to a great Purity of Converſation, that you are forbid all *fooliſh Diſcourſe,* and *filthy Jeſtings,* as expreſly as you are forbid *Swearing,* that you are told to *let no cor-rupt Communication proceed out of your mouth, but ſuch as is good for the uſe of edifying* And yet you go to the *Houſe ſet apart* for corrupt Communications . You hire Perſons to en-tertain you with all manner of *Ribaldry, Prophaneneſs, Rant,* and *Impurity* of Diſcourſe ; who are to preſent you with *vile* Thoughts, and lewd Imaginations, in *fine Language,* and to make *wicked, vain* and *impure Diſcourſe,* more lively and af-fecting, than you could poſſibly have it in any ill Com-pany Now is not this Sinning with as high a Hand, and as groſsly offending againſt plain Doctrines of Scripture, as if you were to give your *Money* to be entertain'd with *Muſical Oaths* and *Curſes ?*

You

You might reasonably think that *Woman* very ridiculous in her *Piety*, that durst not swear her self, but should nevertheless frequent *Places* to hear *Oaths* But you may as justly think her very ridiculous in her *Modesty*, who, tho' she dares not to say, or look, or do an immodest Thing her self, should yet give her *Money* to see *Women* forget the *Modesty* of their Sex, and *talk unpudently* in a Publick *Play-House* If the *Play-House* was fill'd with *Rakes*, and *ill Women*, there would be nothing to be wonder'd at in such an Assembly For *such Persons* to be delighted with such Entertainments, is as natural, as for any *Animal* to delight in its proper *Element* But for Persons who profess Purity and Holiness, who would not be suspected of *immodest* or *corrupt Communications*, for them to come under the Roof of a *House devoted* to such ill Purposes, and to be pleased Spectators of such Actions and Discourses, as are the Pleasures of the most abandon'd Persons, for them to give their Money to be thus entertain'd, is such a Contradiction to all *Piety* and common Sense, as cannot be sufficiently exposed

Consider now, if you please, the Worship of *Images* You wonder that any People can be so blind, so regardless of Scripture, as to comply with such a Devotion It is indeed wonderful But is it not as wonderful, that you should seek and delight in an Entertainment, made up of Lewdness, Prophaneness, and all the extravagant Rant of disorder'd Passions, when the Scripture positively charges you to forbear all *corrupt Communication*, as that which *grieves the Holy Spirit*, and separates him from us? Is not this being *blind*, and *regardless* of Scripture in as high a degree? For how can the Scripture speak higher, or plainer, or enforce its Doctrines with a more dreadful Penalty, than that which is here declared? For, without the Holy Spirit of God, we are but Figures of Christians, and must dye in our Sins

If it was said in Scripture, Forbear from all Image-Worship, because it *grieves and removes the Holy Spirit* from you; perhaps you would think the Worshippers of *Images* under greater Blindness and Corruption of Heart, than they now are But, observe, that if you go to the *Stage*, you offend against Scripture in as high a degree as they, who should worship Images, tho' the Scriptures forbid it, as *grievous to the Holy Spirit*

If therefore I was to rest here, I might fairly say, that I had prov'd the Stage to be as contrary to Scripture, as the Wor-

B   ship

ſhip of *Images* is contrary to the Second Commandment. You think it a ſtrange Contrariety, to ſee People on their Knees before an *Image*, at a Time that the Heart and Mind ſhould raiſe it ſelf to God But then, is it not as ſtrange a Contrariety, that a Perſon ſhould indulge himſelf in the lewd prophane Diſcourſes of the *Stage*, who ſhould have his Heart and Mind preſerv'd in the Wiſdom, the Purity and Spirit of Religion? For an Image is not ſo contrary to God, as Plays are contrary to the Wiſdom, the Purity, and the Spirit of Scripture An Image is only contrary to God, as it has no Power, or Perfection But *Plays* are contrary to Scripture, as the Devil is contrary to God, as they are full of another Spirit and Temper. He therefore that indulges himſelf in the wicked Temper of the *Stage*, ſins againſt as plain Scripture, and offends againſt more Doctrines of it, than he that uſes *Images* in his Devotions

I proceed now to a Third Argument againſt the Stage

When you ſee the *Players* acting with Life and Spirit, Men and Women *equally bold* in all Inſtances of *Prophaneneſs, Paſſion*, and *Immodeſty*, I dare ſay you never ſuſpect any of them to be Perſons of *Chriſtian Piety* You cannot, even in your Imagination, join Piety to ſuch Manners, and ſuch a Way of Life Your Mind will no more allow you to join Piety with the Behaviour of the *Stage*, than it will allow you to think *two* and *two* to be *ten* And perhaps you had rather ſee your Son chained to a *Galley*, or your Daughter driving *Plow*, than getting their Bread on the *Stage*, by adminiſtring in ſo ſcandalous a manner to the Vices and corrupt Pleaſures of the World Let this therefore be another Argument, to prove the *Abſolute Unlawfulneſs* of going to a *Play* For, conſider with your ſelf, Is the Buſineſs of *Players* ſo contrary to Piety, ſo inconſiſtent with the Spirit and Temper of a true Chriſtian, that it is next to a Contradiction to ſuppoſe them united? How then can you take your ſelf to be *innocent*, who *delight in* their Sins, and *hire* them to commit them?

You may make your ſelf a Partaker of other Mens Sins, by Negligence, and for want of reproving them But certainly, if you ſtand by, and aſſiſt Men in their Evil Actions, if you make their Vices your Pleaſures and Entertainment, and pay your Money to be ſo entertained, you make your ſelf a Partaker of their Sins in a very high degree, and conſequent-
ly,

ly, it muſt be as unlawful to go to a *Play*, as it is unlawful to approve, encourage, aſſiſt, and reward a Man for *Renouncing* a Chriſtian Life.

Let therefore every *Man* or *Woman* that goes to a *Play*, ask themſelves this Queſtion, Whether it ſuits with their Religion, to act the *Parts* that are there acted? Perhaps they would think this as inconſiſtent with that degree of Piety that they profeſs, as to do the vileſt Things. But let them conſider, that it muſt be a wicked and unlawful Pleaſure, to delight in any thing that they dare not do themſelves. Let them alſo conſider, that they are really *acting* thoſe *Indecencies* and *Impieties* themſelves, which they think is the particular Guilt of the *Players*. For, a Perſon may very juſtly be ſaid to do that *himſelf*, which he *pays* for the doing, and which is done for his Pleaſure.

You muſt therefore, if you would be conſiſtent with your ſelf, as much abhor the Thoughts of being at a *Play*, as of being a *Player* your ſelf. For, to think that you muſt forbear the one, and not the other, is as abſurd as to ſuppoſe, that you muſt be temperate your ſelf, but may aſſiſt, encourage, and reward other People for their Intemperance. The Buſineſs of a *Player* is prophane, wicked, lewd and immodeſt. To be any way therefore approving, aſſiſting, or encouraging him in ſuch a way of Life, is as evidently ſinful, as it is ſinful to aſſiſt and encourage a Man in *Stealing*, or any other Wickedneſs.

This Argument is not far-fetch'd, or founded in any Subtilties of reaſoning, but is ſo plain and obvious, that the meaneſt Capacity muſt needs underſtand it. I may venture to challenge any one to ſhew me, that the Buſineſs of the *Players* is a more Chriſtian Employment than that of *Robbers*. For he muſt know very little of the Nature of Religion, that can look upon Luſt, Prophaneneſs, and diſorder'd Paſſions, to be leſs contrary to Religion, than the taking Money from the right Owner. And a Perſon who devotes himſelf to this Employment, to get his Bread by gratifying the corrupt Taſte of the World with wanton, wild, prophane Diſcourſes, may be juſtly ſuppos'd to have a more corrupt Heart himſelf, than many a Man who has taken unlawful Ways of relieving his Wants.

I ſpeak to this Matter with thus much Plainneſs, becauſe there is ſo plain Reaſon for it, and becauſe, I think, there is as much Juſtice and Tenderneſs in telling every Player, that his Employment is abominably ſinful, and inconſiſtent with

B 2

the

the Christian Religion, as in telling the same Thing to a *Thief* As it ought to be reckon'd no Sign of Enmity, or Ill-will, if I should attempt to prove to *Malefactors* the horrid Nature of their Sins, and the Necessity of a sincere Repentance, so I hope it will not be look'd upon as any Sign of ill Temper, or Anger at any particular Persons, that I set the Business of Players amongst the most abominable Crimes For, it is with no other Intent, but that they themselves may avoid the dreadful Guilt of so wicked a Profession, and that other People may not dare any longer to support them in it For it certainly concerns all People, who are not so void of Religion as to be Players themselves, to be strictly careful that they have no Share in the Guilt of so unchristian a Profession

This we reckon very good Reasoning in all other Cases A Person that dares not *steal*, thinks it equally sinful to encourage Theft Any one that abhors *Perjury*, or *Murder*, knows that he commits those Sins, if he encourages other People in them What therefore must we think of our selves, if the Blasphemy, Prophaneness, Lewdness, Immodesty, and wicked Rant of Plays, are Parts that we dare not act our selves, yet make it our Diversion to be delighted with those that do? Shall we think our selves more enlighten'd, or more reasonable, than those that worship *Images*? The Second Commandment cannot fright them from the Use of Images, but it is because they have had a superstitious Education, are taught to be blindly obedient, and have the Pretence of Piety for what they do But all the grossest Sins of the *Stage* cannot fright us from it, tho' we see the Sins, and have nothing to pretend for Compliance, but mere Idleness and Diversion

If any one was to collect all the foolish, vain *Devotions*, which poor mistaken Creatures have paid to *Images*, it would sufficiently justify our Abhorrence of them, and shew the Wisdom of the *Reformation* in abolishing the Use of them. But if a Person was to make a Collection of all the wicked, prophane, blasphemous, lewd, impudent, detestable Things, that are said in the Play-House only in *one Season*; it would appear to be such a Mass of Sin, as would sufficiently justify any one in saying, that the Business of Players is the most wicked and detestable Profession in the World

All People therefore who ever enter into their House, or contribute the smallest Mite towards it, must look upon themselves, as having been so far Friends to the most powerful ful

ful Inftruments of Debauchery, and to be guilty of contribu-
ting to a bold, open, and publick Exercife of Impudence,
Impurity, and Prophanenefs   When we encourage any good
Defign, either with our Confent, our Money, or Prefence,
we are apt to take a great deal of Merit to our felves, we
prefently conclude, that we are Partakers of all that is *good
and praife-worthy in it,* of all the Benefit that arifes from it,
becaufe we are Contributors towards it   A Man does not
think that he has no Share in fome publick Charity, becaufe
he is but one in ten thoufand that contributes towards it, but
if it be a religious Charity, and attended with great and happy
Effects, his Confcience tells him that he is a Sharer of *all*
that great Good, to which he contributes   Now let this teach
us, how we ought to judge of the Guilt of encouraging any
thing that is bad, either with our *Confent,* our *Money,* or our
Prefence. We muft not confider how much our fingle Part
contributes towards it, nor how much lefs we contribute than
feveral thoufands of other People, but we muft look at the
whole thing in it felf, and whatever there is of Evil in it, or
whatever Evil arifes from it, we muft charge our felves with
a Share of the whole Guilt of fo great an Evil   Thus it is,
that we hope, and defire to partake of the Merit of all good
Defigns, which we any way countenance and encourage,
and thus it is, that the Guilt of all wicked things which
we countenance and affift, will certainly be laid to our
Charge.

To proceed now to a fourth Argument   When I confider *Churches,* and the Matter of *Divine Service,* that it confifts of holy Readings, Prayers, and Exhortations to Piety,
there is Reafon to think, that the Houfe of God is a natural
Means of promoting Piety and Religion, and rendring Men
devout, and fenfible of their Duty to God   The very Nature of Divine Affemblies thus carried on has this direct Ten-
dency   I ask you whether this is not very plain, that *Churches*
thus employ'd fhould have this Effect? Confider therefore the
Play-Houfe, and the Matter of the Entertainment there, as it
confifts of *Love-Intrigues, blafphemous Paffions, prophane Difcourfes, lewd Defcriptions, filthy Jefts,* and all the moft extravagant Rant of wanton, profligate Perfons of both Sexes,
heating and inflaming one another with all the *Wantonnefs* of
Addrefs, the *Immodefty* of Motion, and *Lewdnefs* of Thought,
that Wit can invent. Confider, I fay, whether it be not plain,
that a Houfe fo employed is as certainly ferving the Caufe of

4

Immo-

Immorality and *Vice*, as the House of God is serving the Cause of *Piety*? For what is there in our *Church Service* that shews it to be *useful* to Piety and Holiness, what is there in Divine Worship to correct and amend the Heart, but what is directly contrary to all that is doing in the *Play-House*? So that one may with the same Assurance affirm, that the *Play-House*, not only when some very prophane Play is on the *Stage*, but in its *daily, common* Entertainments, is as certainly the *House of the Devil*, as the Church is the *House of God* For though the Devil be not professedly worshipp'd by Hymns directed to him, yet most that is there sung is to his Service, he is there *obey'd* and *pleas'd* in as certain a manner, as God is worshipped and honoured in the Church

You must easily see, that this Charge against the *Play-House* is not the Effect of any *particular Temper*, or Weakness of Mind, that it is not an *uncertain Conjecture*, or *religious Whimsy*, but is a Judgment founded as plainly in the *Nature* and *Reason* of things, as when it is affirmed, that the House of God is of Service to Religion And he that absolutely condemns the *Play-House*, as wicked and corrupting, proceeds upon as much Truth and Certainty, as he that absolutely commends the *House of God*, as holy, and tending to promote Piety

When therefore any one pretends to vindicate the *Stage* to you, as a proper Entertainment for holy and religious Persons, you ought to reject the Attempt with as much Abhorrence, as if he should offer to shew you, that our *Church Service* was rightly formed for those Persons to join in, who are *devoted to the Devil* For to talk of the *Lawfulness* and *Usefulness* of the *Stage* is full as absurd, as contrary to the plain Nature of things, as to talk of the Unlawfulness and Mischief of the Service of the Church He therefore that tells you, that you may safely go to the *Play-House*, as an innocent, useful Entertainment of your Mind, commits the same Offence against common Sense, as if he should tell you, that it was dangerous to attend at Divine Service, and that its Prayers and Hymns were great *Pollutions* of the Mind

For the Matter and Manner of *Stage Entertainments* is as undeniable a Proof, and as obvious to common Sense, that the House belongs to the Devil, and is the Place of his Honour, as the Matter and Manner of *Church Service* proves that the Place is appropriated to God

Observe therefore, That as you do not want the Assistance of any one, to shew you the *Usefulness* and *Advantage* of

Divine

Divine Service, becauſe the thing is plain, and ſpeaks for it ſelf, ſo neither, on the other hand, need you any one to ſhew the *Unlawfulneſs* and *Miſchief* of the Stage, becauſe there the thing is equally plain, and ſpeaks for it ſelf So that you are to conſider your ſelf as having the ſame Aſſurance, that the *Stage* is wicked, and to be abhorred and avoided by all Chriſtians, as you have, that the Service of the Church is holy, and to be ſought after by all Lovers of Holineſs Conſider therefore, that your Conduct, with relation to the *Stage*, is not a Matter of *Nicety*, or *ſcrupulous Exactneſs*, but that you are as certain that you do wrong in as notorious a manner, when you go to the *Play-Houſe*, as you are certain that you do right, when you go to *Church*

Now it is of mighty Uſe to conceive things in a right manner, and to ſee them as they are in their own Nature Whilſt you conſider the Play-Houſe only as a *Place of Diverſion*, it may perhaps give no Offence to your Mind There is nothing *ſhocking* in the Thought of it; but if you would lay aſide this Name of it for a while, and conſider it in its *own Nature*, as it really is, you would find that you are as much deceiv'd, if you conſider the *Play-Houſe* as only a *Place of Diverſion*, as you would be, if you conſidered the Houſe of God, only as a Place of *Labour*

When therefore you are tempted to go to a *Play*, either from your own Inclination, or from the Deſire of a Friend, fancy that you was asked in plain Terms to go to the Place of the *Devil's Abode*, where he holds his *filthy Court* of evil Spirits, that you was asked to join in an Entertainment, where he was at the Head of it, where the whole of it was in order to his Glory, that Mens Hearts and Minds might be ſeparated from God, and plunged into all the Pollutions of Sin and Brutality Fancy that you are going to a Place that as certainly belongs to the Devil, as the *heathen Temples* of old, where *Brutes* were worſhipped, where *wanton Hymns* were ſung to *Venus*, and drunken Songs to the God of Wine. Fancy that you are as certainly going to the Devil's *Triumph*, as if you was going to thoſe *old Sports*, where People committed Murder, and offered Chriſtians to be devoured by wild Beaſts, for the Diverſion of the Spectators Now whilſt you conſider the *Play-Houſe* in this View, I ſuppoſe you can no more go to a *Play*, than you can renounce your Chriſtianity

Conſi-

Confider now therefore, that you have not been frighting your felf with *groundlefs Imaginations*; but that which you have heie fancy'd of the *Play-Houfe* is as ftrictly true, as if you had been fancying, that when you go to Church, you go to the Houfe of God, where the heavenly Hoft attend upon his Service, and that when you read the Scriptures, and fing holy Hymns, you join with the Choirs above, and do God's Will on Earth, as it is done in Heaven   For obferve, I pray you, how juftly that Opinion of the *Play-Houfe* is founded For was it a Joy to him to fee *Idols* worfhipped, to fee Hymns and Adorations offer'd up to impure and filthy Deities? Were Places and Feftivals appointed for fuch Ends, juftly efteemed Places and Feftivals devoted to the Devil? Now give the Reafon why all this was juftly reckon'd a Service to the Devil, and you will give as good a Reafon, why the *Play-Houfe* is to be efteemed his *Temple*

For what though Hymns and Adorations are not offer'd to impure and filthy Deities, yet if *Impurity* and *Filthinefs* is the *Entertainment*, if immodeft Songs, prophane Rant, if Luft and Paffion entertain the Audience, the Bufinefs is the fame, and the Affembly does the *fame Honour* to the Devil, though they be not gather'd together in the Name of fome *Heathen God*

For Impurity and Prophanenefs in the Woifhippers of the True God, is as acceptable a Service to the Devil, as Impurity and Prophanenefs in Idolaters, and peihaps a *lewd Song*, in an Affembly of Chriftians, gives him a greatei Delight, than in a Congregation of *Heathens*

If therefore we may fay, that a *Houfe* or *Feftival* was the Devil's, becaufe he was *delighted* with it, becaufe what was theie done, was an *acceptable Service* to him; we may be affured, that the *Play-Houfe* is as really the Houfe of the Devil, as any other Houfe ever was   Nay, it is reafonable to think, that the *Play-Houfes* in this Kingdom are a gieatei Pleafure to him, than any *Temple* he evei had in the Heathen World.   For, as it is a greater Conqueft, to make the Difciples of Chrift delight in *Lewdnefs* and *Prophanenefs*, than ignorant Heathen, fo a *Houfe* that, in the Midft of *Chriftian Churches*, trains up Chriftians to *Lewdnefs* and *Prophanenefs*, that makes the Worfhippers of Chrift flock together in Crowds, to rejoice in an Entertainment that is as contrary to the Spirit of Chrift, as *Hell* is contrarary to *Heaven*   A Houfe fo employ'd, may juftly be reckon'd a more delightful Habitation of the Devil, than any Temple in the Heathen World.

When

When therefore you go to the *Play-House*, you have as much Affurance that you go to the Devil's peculiar Habitation, that you fubmit to his Defigns, and rejoice in his Diverfions, (which are his beft Devices againft Chriftianity) you have as much Affurance of this, as that they who worfhipped filthy Deities, were in reality Worfhippers of the Devil.

Hence it appears, that if inftead of confidering the Play-Houfe as only a Place of Diverfion, you will but examine what Materials it is made of, if you will but confider the Nature of the Entertainment, and what is there doing, you will find it as wicked a Place, as finful a Diverfion, and as truly the peculiar Pleafure of the Devil, as any wicked Place, or finful Diverfion in the Heathen World When therefore you are asked to go to a Play, don't think that you are only asked to go to a Diverfion, but be affured that you are asked to *yield* to the Devil, to go over to his Party, and to make one of his Congregation That if you do go, you have not only the Guilt of *buying* fo much vain Communication, and paying People for being wicked, but are alfo as certainly guilty of going to the Devil's Houfe, and doing him the fame Honour, as if you was to partake of fome *Heathen Feftival*. You muft confider, that all the Laughter there is not only vain and foolifh, but that it is a Laughter amongft Devils, that you are upon prophane Ground, and hearing Mufick in the very Porch of Hell

Thus it is in the Reafon of the thing, and if we fhould now confider the State of our *Play-Houfe*, as it is in Fact, we fhould find it anfwering all thefe Characters, and producing Effects fuitable to its Nature But I fhall forbear this Confideration, it being as unneceffary to tell the Reader, that our *Play-Houfe* is in Fact the *Sink of Corruption and Debauchery*; that it is the general Rendezvous of the moft profligate Perfons of both Sexes, that it corrupts the Air, and turns the adjacent Places into publick Nufances, this is as unneceffary, as to tell him that the *Exchange* is a Place of *Merchandife*

Now it is to be obferv'd, that this is not the State of the *Play-Houfe* through any accidental Abufe, as any innocent or good thing may be abufed, but that Corruption and Debauchery are the truly natural and genuine Effects of the *Stage-Entertainment* Let not therefore any one fay, that he is not anfwerable for thofe Vices and Debaucheries which are occafion'd by the *Play-Houfe*, for fo far as he partakes of

C

the

the Pleasure of the *Stage*, and is an Encourager of it, so far he is chargeable with those Disorders which necessarily are occasion'd by it. If Evil arises from our doing our Duty, or our Attendance at any *good Design*, we are not to be frighted at it, but if Evil arises from any thing as its *natural* and *genuine* Effect, in all such Cases, so far as we contribute to the Cause, so far we make our selves guilty of the Effects. So that all who any way assist the *Play-House*, or ever encourage it by their Presence, make themselves chargeable, in some degree, with all the Evils and Vices which follow from it. Since therefore it cannot be doubted by any one, whether the *Play-House* be a Nursery of Vice and Debauchery, since the evil Effects it has upon People's Manners is as visible as the Sun at Noon, one would imagine that all People of *Virtue* and *Modesty* should not only avoid it, but avoid it with the utmost Abhorrence, that they should be so far from entring into it, that they should detest the very Sight of it. For what a Contradiction is it to common Sense, to hear a Woman lamenting the miserable Lewdness and Debauchery of the Age, the vicious Taste and irregular Pleasures of the World, and at the same time dressing herself to meet the lewdest Part of the World at the Fountain-head of all Lewdness, and making herself one of that Crowd, where every abandon'd Wretch is glad to be present? She may fancy that she hates and abominates their Vices, but she may depend upon it, that till she hates and abominates the Place of vicious Pleasures, till she dare not come near an Entertainment, which is the Cause of so great Debauchery, and the Pleasure of the most debauched People, till she is thus disposed, she wants the truest Sign of a real and religious Abhorrence of the Vices of the Age.

For, to wave all other Considerations, I would only ask her a Question or two on the single Article of *Modesty*. What is Modesty? Is it a little *mechanical outside* Behaviour, that goes no farther than a few *Forms* and *Modes* at particular Times and Places? Or is it a *real Temper*, a natural Disposition of the Heart, that is founded in *Religion*? Now if Modesty is only a mechanical Observance of a little outside Behaviour, then I can easily perceive how a modest Woman may frequent *Plays*, there is no Inconsistency for such a one to be one thing in one Place, and another in another Place, to disdain an immodest Conversation, and yet at the same time, relish and delight in immodest and impudent Speeches in a publick *Play-House*. But if Modesty is a *real Temper*

and

and Difposition of the Heart, that is founded in the Princi-
ples of Religion, then I confefs I cannot comprehend, how
a Perfon of fuch Modefty fhould ever come twice into the
Play-Houfe   For if it is Reafon and Religion that has in-
fpired her with a modeft Heart, that makes her careful of her
Behaviour, that makes her hate and abhor every Word, or
Look, or Hint in Converfation, that has the Appearance of
Lewdnefs, that makes her fhun the Company of fuch as talk
with too much Freedom   If fhe is thus modeft in *common
Life*, from a Principle of Religion, a Temper of Heart, is it
poffible for fuch a one (I don't fay to feek) but to bear
with the Immodefty and Impudence of the *Stage* ? For muft
not Immodefty and Impudence, muft not loofe and wanton
Difcourfe be the fame *hateful things*, and give the fame Offence to a modeft Mind, in one Place as in another ? And
muft not that Place, which is the Seat of Immodefty, where
Men and Women are trained up in Lewdnefs, where almoft
every Day in the Year is a Day devoted to the foolifh Reprefentations of *Rant, Luft,* and *Paffion*, muft not fuch a
Place of all others be the moft odious to a Mind, that is
truly modeft upon Principles of *Reafon* and *Religion* ? One
would fuppofe that fuch a Perfon fhould as much abominate
the Place, as any other filthy Sight, and be as much offended with an Invitation to it, as if fhe was invited to fee an
immodeft Picture   For the Reprefentations of the *Stage,* the
inflamed Paffions of Lovers there defcrib'd, are as grofs an
Offence to the Ear, as any Reprefentation that can offend the
Eye

It ought not to be concluded, that becaufe I affirm the
Play-Houfe to be an Entertainment *contrary* to Modefty, that
therefore I accufe all People as void of Modefty, who ever
go to it   I might affirm, that *Tranfubftantiation* is contrary
to all *Senfe* and *Reafon*, but then it would be a wrong Con-
clufion, to fay that I affirmed, that all who believe it are void
of all *Senfe* and *Reafon*

Now, as *Prejudices,* the Force of *Education,* the Authority
of *Number,* the Way of the World, the Example of *great
Names,* may make People *believe,* fo the fame Caufes may
make People act againft *all Senfe and Reafon,* and be guilty
of Practices, which no more fuit with the *Purity* of their Religion, than *Tranfubftantiation* agrees with *common Senfe*

To proceed.   *Trebonia* thus excufes herfelf for going to
the *Play-Houfe*   I go but feldom ; and then either with my
C 2   *Mothers*

Mother, or my *Aunt* We always know the Play before-hand, and never go on the *Sacrament*-Week And what harm, pray, fays fhe, can there be in this? It breaks in upon no Rules of my Life. I neglect no Part of my Duty I go to *Church*, and perform the fame Devotions at home, as on other Days

It ought to be obferved, that this Excufe can only be allow'd, where the Diverfion it felf is innocent It muft therefore firft be confider'd, what the Entertainment is in it felf; whether it be fuitable to the Spirit and Temper of Religion: For, if it is right and proper in it felf, it needs no Excufe; but if it be *wrong*, and *contrary* to Religion, we are not to ufe it *cautioufly*, but to avoid it *conftantly*

Trebonia muft be told, that it is no Proof of the Innocency of a Thing, that it does not interfere with her *Hours of Duty*, nor break the Regularity of her Life, for, very wicked Ways of fpending Time, may yet be confiftent with a regular Diftribution of our Hours. She muft therefore confider, not only whether fuch a Diverfion hinders the Regularity of her Life, or breaks in upon her Hours of Devotion, publick or private, but whether it hinders, or any way affects the *Spirit* and *Temper*, which all her Devotions afpire after Is it conformable to that heavenly Affection, that Love of God, that Purity of Heart, that Wifdom of Mind, that Perfection of Holinefs, that Contempt of the World, that Watchfulnefs and Self-denial, that Humility and Fear of Sin, which Religion requireth? Is it conformable to thefe Graces, which are to be the *daily Subject* of all her Prayers? This is the only way for her to know the *Innocency* of going to a Play If what fhe there hears and fees, has no *Contrariety* to any *Grace* or *Virtue* that fhe prays for, if all that there paffes, be fit for the *Purity* and *Piety* of one that is led by the Spirit of Chrift, and is *working out* her *Salvation with fear and trembling*, if the Stage be an Entertainment, that may be thought to be according to the Will of God, then fhe difpofes of an Hour very innocently, tho' her *Mother* or her *Aunt* were not with her.

But if the *contrary* to all this be true, if moft of what fhe there *hears* and *fees*, be as contrary to the *Piety* and *Purity* of Chriftianity, as *Feafting* is contrary to *Fafting*; if the *Houfe* which fhe fupports with her *Money*, and encourages with her *Prefence*, be a notorious Means of Corruption, vifibly carrying on the Caufe of *Vice* and *Debauchery*; fhe muft not think her felf excus'd for being with her *Mother*.

Trebo-

Trebonia would perhaps think it strange, to hear one of her virtuous Acquaintance giving the like Reason for going now and then to a *Masquerade*

Now, this Diversion is new in our Country, and therefore most People *yet* judge of it in the manner that they ought, because they are not blinded by *Use and Custom*. But let any one give but the true Reasons, why a Person of Virtue and Piety should not go to *Masquerades*, and the same Reasons will as plainly shew, that Persons of Virtue and Piety should keep at as great a distance from the *Play-House*. For, the Entertainment of the *Stage* is more directly opposite to the Purity of Religion, than *Masquerades*, and is besides as certain a Means of Corruption, and serves all bad Ends in as great a degree as they do. They only differ, as bad Things of the same Kind may differ from one another So that if the evil Use, and ill Consequences of *Masquerades*, be a sufficient Reason to deter People of Piety from partaking of them, the same evil Use, and ill Consequences of the *Stage*, ought to keep all People of Virtue from it If People will consult their *Tempers* only, they may take the Entertainment of one, and condemn the other, as following the same Guide, they may abhor *Intemperance*, and indulge *Malice*: But if they will consult Religion, and make that the Ground of their Opinions, they will find more and stronger Reasons for a *Constant Abhorrence* of the *Stage*, than of *Masquerades*.

Again If *Trebonia* should hear a Person excusing her Use of *Paint* in this manner, That truly she painted but *very seldom*, that she always said her Prayers first, that she never us'd it on *Sundays*, or the Week before the *Communion* · *Trebonia* would pity such a *Mixture* of Religion and Weakness She would desire her to use her Reason, and either to allow *Painting* to be innocent, suitable to the *Sobriety* and *Humility* of a Christian, or else to think it as unlawful at one Time, as at another. But, *Trebonia*, would you not think it still stranger, that she should condemn *Painting* as *odious* and *sinful*, and yet think that the *Regularity* of her Life, and the *Exactness* of her Devotions, might make it lawful for her to paint *now and then* ?

I don't doubt but you plainly see the Weakness and Folly of such a Pretence for *Painting*, under such Rules, at certain Times And if you would but as impartially consider your Pretences for going sometimes to the Play-House, under the same Rules, you would certainly find them more weak and

and unreasonable   For *Painting* may with more Reason be reckoned an *innocent Ornament*, than the Play-House an *innocent Diversion*   And it suppofes a greater *Vanity* of Mind, a more *perverted* Judgment, and a deeper Corruption of Heart, to feek the Diverfion of the *Stage*, than to take the Pleafure of a *borrow'd Colour*   Painting, when confider'd in it felf, is undoubtedly a great Sin, but when it is compared to the Ufe of the Stage, it is but as the *Mote* compared to the *Beam*.

I know you are offended at this *Comparifon*, becaufe you judge by your *Temper* and *Prejudices*, and don't confider the things as they are in themfelves, by the pure Light of *Reafon* and *Religion*   Painting has not been the way of your Family, it is fuppos'd to be the Practice but of *very few*, and thofe who ufe it, endeavour to *conceal* it   this makes you readily condemn it.   On the contrary, your *Mother* and your *Aunt* carry you to the *Play*, you fee *virtuous* People there, and the fame Perfons that fill our *Churches*, fo that your *Temper* is as much engaged to think it lawful to go fometimes to a *Play*, as it is engaged to think the Ufe of *Paint* always odious and finful.

Lay afide therefore thefe Prejudices for a while, and fancy that you had been trained up in fome Corner of the World in the Principles of Chriftianity, and had never heard either of the *Play-Houfe* or *Painting*.   Imagine now that you was to examine the Lawfulnefs of them by the Doctrines of Scripture, you would firft defire to be told the Nature of thefe things, and what they meant   You would be told, that *Painting* was the borrowing of *Colours* from Art, to make the Face look more beautiful   Now tho' you found no exprefs Text of Scripture againft *Painting*, you would find that it was exprefly againft Tempers required in Scripture, you would therefore condemn it, as proceeding from a Vanity of Mind, and Fondnefs of Beauty   You would fee that the Harm of Painting confifted in this, that it proceeded from a Temper of Mind contrary to the Sobriety and Humility of a Chriftian, which indeed is harm enough, becaufe this Humility and Sobriety of Mind is as effential to Religion, as Charity and Devotion   So that in judging according to Scripture, you would hold it as unreafonable to *paint fometimes*, as to be fometimes *malicious, indevout, proud,* or *falfe*

You are now to confider the *Stage*, you are to keep clofe to Scripture, and fancy that you yet know nothing of *Plays*   You ask therefore firft, what the *Stage* or *Play-Houfe* is? You

are

are told that it is a *Place* where all forts of People meet to be entertain'd with *Difcourfes, Actions,* and *Reprefentations,* which are recommended to the Heart by beautiful Scenes, the Splendor of Lights, and the Harmony of Mufick. You are told that thefe Difcourfes are the Invention of Men of Wit and Imagination, which defcribe imaginary *Intrigues* and *Scenes* of *Love,* and introduce *Men* and *Women* difcourfing, raving, and acting in all the wild, indecent Tranfports of *Luft* and *Paffion.* You are told, that the Diverfion partly confifts of *lewd* and *prophane* Songs fung to fine Mufick, and partly of extravagant Dialogues between *immodeft Perfons* talking in a Stile of *Love* and *Madnefs,* that is no where elfe to be found, and entertaining the *Chriftian Audience* with all the Violence of Paffion, Corruption of Heart, Wantonnefs of Mind, Immodefty of Thought, and prophane Jefts, that the Wit of the *Poet* is able to invent. You are told, that the *Players,* Men and Women, are trained up to act and reprefent all the Defcriptions of Luft and Paffion in the *livelieft manner,* to add a Lewdnefs of Action to lewd Speeches, that they get their Live'lhood by *Curfing, Swearing,* and *Ranting* for three Hours together to an Affembly of *Chriftians.*

Now though you find no particular Text of Scripture condemning the *Stage,* or *Tragedy* or *Comedy,* in exprefs Words, yet what is much more, you find that fuch Entertainments are a grofs Contradiction to the *whole Nature* of Religion, they are not contrary to this or that particular Temper, but are contrary to that *whole Turn of Heart* and *Mind* which Religion requires. Painting is contrary to *Humility,* and therefore is to be avoided as finful, but the Entertainment of the *Stage,* as it confifts of *blafphemous* Expreffions, *wicked* Speeches, *fwearing, curfing,* and *prophaning* the Name of God, as it abounds with *impious* Rant, *filthy* Jefts, *diftracted* Paffions, grofs Defcriptions of *Luft,* and *wanton Songs,* is a *Contradiction to every Doctrine* that our Saviour and his Apoftles have taught us. So that to abhor *Painting* at all times, becaufe it fuppofes a Vanity of Mind, and is contrary to Humility, and yet think there is a lawful Time to go to the *Play-Houfe,* is as contrary to common Senfe, as if a Man fhould hold that it was lawful fometimes to offend againft *all the Doctrines* of Religion, and yet always unlawful to offend againft *any one* Doctrine of Religion.

If therefore you was to come (as I fuppofed) from fome Corner of the World, where you had been ufed to live and

judge

judge by the Rules of Religion, and upon your Arrival here, had been told, what Painting and the *Stage* was, as you would not expect to see Persons of *religious Humility* carrying their Daughters to *Paint-Shops*, or inviting their pious Friends to go along with them, so much less would you expect to hear, that *devout, pious* and *modest* Women carried their Daughters, and invited their virtuous Friends to meet them at the Play. Least of all could you imagine, that there were any People too *pious* and *devout*, to indulge the Vanity of *Painting*, and yet *not* devout and pious enough, to abhor the Immodesty, Prophaneness, Ribaldry, Immorality, and Blasphemy of the *Stage*.

To proceed   A *polite Writer* (*a*) of a late Paper thought he had sufficiently ridiculed a certain Lady's Pretensions to *Piety*, when, speaking of her *Closet*, he says,

> *Together lie her Prayer-Book and Paint,*
> *At once t' improve the Sinner and the Saint.*

Now, whence comes it that this Writer judges so rightly, and speaks the Truth so plainly, in the Matter of Painting? Whence comes it, that the Generality of his Readers think his Observation just, and join with him in it? It is because Painting is not yet an *acknowledg'd Practice*, but is for the most part reckon'd a *shameful Instance* of Vanity   Now, as we are not prejudiced in favour of this Practice, and have no Excuses to make for our *own Share* in it, so we judge of it impartially, and immediately perceive its Contrariety to a Religious *Temper* and *State* of Mind.   This *Writer* saw this in so strong a Light, that he does not scruple to suppose, that *Paint* is as natural and proper a Means to improve the *Sinner*, as the Prayer-Book is to improve the Saint.

I should therefore hope, that it need not be imputed to any *Sowreness* of Temper, Religious *Weakness*, or *Dulness* of Spirits, if a *Clergyman* should imagine, that the *Prophaneness, Debauchery, Lewdness*, and *Blasphemy* of the *Stage*, is as natural a Means to improve the *Sinner*, as a *Bottle of Paint*   or if he should venture to shew, that the *Church* and the *Play-House* are as ridiculous a Contradiction, and do no more suit with the *same* Person, than the *Prayer-Book and Paint*.

(*a*) *Spectat.* N° 79.

I shall

I shall now make a Reflexion or two upon the present celebrated Entertainment of the *Stage*, which is so much to the Taste of this Christian Country, that it has been acted almost every Night this whole Season, I mean *Apollo* and *Daphne*

The first Scene is said to be, a *magnificent Palace discover'd · Venus attended with Graces and Pleasures*

Now how is it possible, that such a Scene as this should be fit for the Entertainment of Christians ? Can *Venus* and her *Graces* and *Pleasures* talk any Language that is *like* themselves, but what must be *unlike* to the Spirit of Christianity ? The very proposing such a Scene as this, supposes the Audience to be fit for the Entertainment of *Lust* and *Wantonness*. For what else can *Venus* and her *Pleasures* offer to them ? Had we any thing of the Spirit of Christianity in us, or were earnestly desirous of those holy Tempers, which are to render us pure in the Eyes of God, we should abominate the very Proposal of such a Scene as this, as knowing that it must be an Entertainment fitter for *publick Stews*, than for People who make any Pretences to the Holiness and Purity of the Spirit of Christ   The Scripture saith, *Mortify therefore your members which are upon earth, fornication, uncleanness, inordinate affection, evil concupiscence*   This is the Religion by which we are to be saved   But can the Wit of Man invent any thing more contrary to this, than an Entertainment from *Venus* attended with her *Pleasures* ? That People should have such a Religion as this, and at the same time such an Entertainment, is an astonishing Instance of the Degeneracy of the present State of Christianity amongst us.   For if the first Scene had been the *Devil attended with Fiends, cursing and blaspheming*, no one could shew that such a Scene was more contrary to the Religion of *Christians*, than a Scene with *Venus* and her *Pleasures*.   And if the Devil himself had been consulted by our *Stage-Wits*, which of these Scenes he had rather have, he would certainly have chosen *Venus* and her *Pleasures*, as much fitter to debauch and corrupt a Christian Audience, than a Scene of *cursing* and *blaspheming*.

The Scripture thus describeth the Infatuation of the old Idolaters. *And none considereth in his heart neither is there knowledge, nor understanding to say, I have burnt part of it in the fire, yea, I have also baked bread upon the coals thereof, and shall I make the residue thereof an abomination ? Shall*

D   *I fall*

I fall down to the Stock of a Tree? * It is here reckon'd a strange Instance of their Blindness, that they did not make so easy a Reflexion upon the nature of things But how near are we to this Blindness, if we don't make as easy a Reflexion upon this Entertainment; for the very mentioning of such a *Scene* as this, is as plain a Demonstration, that the Entertainment is contrary to our Religion, as the *burning* of Wood, and its falling into *Ashes,* is a Demonstration that Wood is of a Nature contrary to God. How are we therefore more enlighten'd, if none of us considereth in his Heart, neither is there Knowledge, nor Understanding in us to say, *These are the filthy Deities of the Devil's Invention, with which he polluted and defiled the Heathen World; and shall we still preserve their Power amongst us? Shall we make such Abominations our Diversion?*

For if we worship the God of *Purity,* if we cannot worship him but with Hearts devoted to Purity, what have we to do with these Images of Lewdness? If we dress a *Venus,* and celebrate her Power, and make her *Graces* and *Pleasures* meet us in wanton *Forms,* and wanton *Language* , is it not as absurd, as contrary to our Religion, as to set up a *Baal,* in the Temple of God? What greater Contradiction is there, either to Reason or Religion, in one Case than in the other? *Baal* is as fit for our Devotions, as *Venus* is for our Rejoycings and Praises.

So that the very naming of such a Scene as this is *unlawful Language,* and carries as great a Contrariety to our Religion, as the Worship of *Baal*

Here two Women (whom I suppose to be baptiz'd Christians) represent *Venus* and *Diana* in this Language.

Ven   *Am'rous Kisses,*
Dian.   *Nuptial Blisses,*
      { *Lovers Pleasures,*
      { *Cupid's Treasures,*
      { *Are the Sweets that Life improve.*

Now if a common *Prostitute* was to come drunk out of a *Brandy Shop* singing these Words, she would act like herself. No one could say that she had forgot her Character, or was *singing* one way, and *living* another. And I dare say, there

---

* *Isa* 44 19.

is

is no *Rake* in the Audience so debauch'd, as not to think this a sufficient Celebration of the Praises and Happiness of his Pleasures.

But what do other People do here? Is there any Entertainment in this Place for *pious, sober,* and *devout* Minds? Does it become them to sing the Praises of Debauchery, or sit amongst those that do?

When we hear of a *Witches Feast,* we don't hear of any but *Witches* that go to it. The Mirth and Joy of such Meetings is left wholly to themselves. Now if these impudent Celebrations of *Venus* and her *Pleasures* were left wholly to *Rakes* and *Prostitutes*, if we reckon'd it an Entertainment as contrary to Religion, as a *Witches Feast*, it would only shew, that we judged as rightly in one Case, as in the other. And indeed, one would think, that no Christian need be told, that *Venus* and her *Graces* are as much the Devil's *Machinery*, as *Witches* and *Imps*.

To proceed.

If a Person in Conversation was to address himself to a *Modest* Lady in these words, *Am'rous Kisses,* &c she would think herself very ill used, and that she ought to resent such Treatment. She would think, that her *Modesty* might well be question'd, if she bore such Language.

But how it is consistent with such Modesty, to hire People to entertain her with the same Language in Publick, is a Difficulty not easily to be explain'd. Can *Fathers* and *Mothers,* who sit here with their Children, recommend Purity to them at home, when they have carry'd them to hear the Praises of Lewdness, as the *Sweets which Life improve?*

If a Person was to make a publick Harangue in favour of *Image-Worship,* telling us, that it was the finest Means of raising the Heart to a Delight in God, we should think him a *very wicked Man,* and that the Ears and Hearts of Christians ought to detest such Discourses. Yet Christian People can meet in Crowds, and give their Money to have this repeated in their Ears, that *Am'rous Kisses, Lovers Pleasures,* Cupid's *Treasures, are the Sweets which Life improve.* This, it seems, is no *Idolatry*.

We are told in Scripture, that *Covetousness* is *Idolatry,* and the Reason is, because it alienates the Heart from God, and makes it rest in something else. The covetous Man is an *Idolater,* because his Heart says, that *Gain* and *Bags* of Gold are the *Sweets which Life improve.* And can we think that

D 2   that

that corrupt Heart, that celebrates *Luſt* and *Wantonneſs*, as the *Sweets which Life improve*, is guilty of *leſs Idolatry*, than he that ſays the ſame thing of *Riches*? As ſure as there is ſuch a Sin as *Idolatry*, as ſure as the ſordid *Miſer* is guilty of it, ſo ſure is it that theſe words are chargeable, not only with exceſſive *Immodeſty*, but plain *Idolatry*. For how do we think that the *Pagans* worſhipp'd *Venus*? We cannot ſuppoſe that it was with *Faſting* and *Prayer*, or any *ſerious* Devotions. No, they paid her ſuch a Devotion, as the *Stage* now does, they call'd upon her in *lewd* Songs, and prais'd her, in praiſing the Pleaſures of Luſt and Impurity, in rejoicing in her mighty Power, and celebrating her Pleaſures, as the true *Sweets which Life improve*.

These Women go on thus.

> Dian *Still to languiſh*
> Ven. *With ſweet Anguiſh,*
>   { *Softly ſighing,*
>   { *Murm'ring, dying,*
>   { *Are th' immortal Gifts of Love.*

Here Muſick and Voices, as wanton as the Words, are employ'd to make a deeper Impreſſion on the Hearts of the Audience. Here enter *Bacchus, Pan,* and *Silenus,* attended with *Satyrs, Fawns* and *Sylvans.*

And indeed, they enter very properly, for the Diſcourſe is very agreeable to their Nature. But what have Chriſtians to do with this Company? Do they come here to *renounce* their Religion? Or can they think that this Society, with the moſt beaſtly *Images* that the Heathen World could invent, is a Society that they may partake of, without *Renouncing* Chriſt?

Our Religion chargeth us, not to *keep company, if any one that is called a Brother, be a fornicator,* * &c. But where have we left our Religion, if we not only company with People devoted to Impurity, but make their Company our Delight, and *hire* them to entertain us with all the lewd Imaginations that can be invented? If we are not content with this, but *conjure* up all the impure *Fictions* of the Heathen

---

* 1 Cor 5 11

World, and make their *imaginary Deities* more vile and wanton than ever they made them, to render them agreeable to our Chriſtian Minds, ſhall we reckon this amongſt our *ſmall Sins*? Shall we think it a pardonable Infirmity, to partake of ſuch an Entertainment as this?

The Apoſtle ſaith, *Ye cannot drink the Cup of the Lord, and the Cup of Devils   Ye cannot be partakers of the Lord's Table, and the Table of Devils* * And can we think that we are not drinking the Cup of Devils, or that we are not at the Devil's Table, when his moſt favourite Inſtruments of Impiety, *Venus, Bacchus, Silenus, Satyrs* and *Fawns*, are the Company that we meet to be entertain'd with? If this is not being at the Devil's Table, he had no Table in the Heathen World   For ſurely, they who call up Devils to their Entertainment, who cannot be enough delighted, unleſs the impious Dæmons of the Heathen World converſe with them, are in a ſtricter Communication with the Devil, than they who only eat of that Meat which had been offer'd in Sacrifice

Our bleſſed Saviour ſaith, *He that looketh upon a woman, to luſt after her, hath already committed adultery with her in his heart*   Can we reckon our ſelves his Diſciples, who hire our Fellow-Chriſtians, and Chriſtian Women, (whoſe chief Ornament is a ſincere Modeſty) to ſing in merry Aſſemblies ſuch Words as theſe   *Still to languiſh, with ſweet Anguiſh ; Softly ſighing, murm'ring, dying, Are th' immortal Gifts of Love?*

Who can ſay that I carry Matters too high, when I call this, *renouncing* Chriſtianity? For, can any Words be more expreſsly contrary to the Doctrine of our Saviour, and that in ſo important a Point? And does not he ſufficiently renounce Chriſtianity, who renounces ſo great a Doctrine, that has Chriſt for its Author?

If we were to make a Jeſt of the *Sacraments* in our merry Aſſemblies, we ſhould ſhew as much Regard to Chriſtianity, as by ſuch Diſcourſes as theſe   For all *lewd Diſcourſes* are as plainly contrary to eſſential Doctrines of Scripture, as any Ridicule upon the Sacraments that can be invented   It may be you could not ſit in the *Play-Houſe*, if you ſaw *Baptiſm* made a Jeſt of, and its Uſe reproach'd   But pray, why

---

* 1 Cor 10 21.

don't you think that there *is* as much *Prophaneness* and *Irreligion* in impudent Speeches and Songs? Has not Christ said as much about *Purity* of Heart, as about either of the *Sacraments?* Has not he made Chastity of Heart as necessary to Salvation, as the Sacraments? How comes it then, that an impudent Praise of Lust and Wantonness is not as *prophane*, as a Ridicule upon the Sacraments? What Rule of Reason or Religion do you go by, when you think it highly sinful to sit and hear the *Sacraments* jested upon, and yet are chearful and delighted with such Songs and Discourses, as ridicule *Chastity* of Heart, and religious *Modesty?* Can you suppose, that in the Eyes of God you appear as a better Christian, than those who make merry with prophaning the Sacraments? If you can think this, you must hold that the Sacraments are more essential to Religion than *Purity* of Heart, and that it is more acceptable to God to *wash*, than to be *clean*, more pleasing to him to treat the *Altar* as holy, than to live in *Holiness* of Heart

The Sacraments have nothing valuable in their own Nature, they are only useful to Christians, and to be treated with Reverence, because Christ has appointed them as Means of Holiness. But Purity and Chastity of Heart is an essential and internal Excellence, that by its own Nature perfects the Soul, and renders it more acceptable to God To abhor therefore a Jest upon the *Sacraments*, and yet divert our selves with *impure* Rant, and *lewd* Songs, is being like those who *abhor Idols*, and yet *commit Sacrilege*

All therefore who partake of this sinful Entertainment, who take their Share of Mirth in such Scenes of Impurity and Lewdness, must look upon themselves not only as Offenders against the Laws of *Purity*, but also as chargeable with such *Irreligion* and *Prophaneness*, as they are, who are merry in such Meetings as ridicule and banter the Use of the Holy Sacraments

It is a great Aggravation of the Guilt of these Assemblies, that Women are employ'd to lay aside the peculiar Ornament of their Sex, and to add an Immodesty of Action and Address to immodest Speeches If we knew of an Assembly, where Clergymen met to ridicule the *sacred Rites* of Religion for the sake of entertaining the Audience with *Eloquence*, if we should find that great Part of the Audience were *Clergymen*, who could not forbear an Entertainment so contrary to their Profession, it would easily be seen, that such a sinful

Enter-

Entertainment was more unreasonable, because Clergymen acted in it, and Clergymen came to be entertain'd with it.

Now this is the Case of the Stage-Entertainment, Women are as particularly called to a *singular Modesty*, as Clergymen are to the Duties of their Profession; if therefore Women act Parts in lewd and impudent Entertainments, they have as much forgot themselves, and appear as *detestable*, as Clergymen that talk *prophanely*. And if other Women come to delight themselves with seeing their *Sisters* acting so contrary to themselves, and the peculiar Duties of their Condition, they as much forget themselves, as those *Clergy* who should meet to see their *Brethren* raise Diversion out of *Prophaneness*. When therefore virtuous and prudent Women think they may go to the *Stage*, where Women so openly depart from the Decencies which are necessary to their Sex, let them consider what they would think of such virtuous and prudent Divines, as should meet to see Clergymen openly contradict the Duties of their sacred Office For it is the same Absurdity, for modest Women to take pleasure in a Diversion, where Women are *immodest*, as for a good Clergyman to be pleas'd with a Meeting, where Clergymen are *prophane* This must be own'd to be strictly true, unless it can be shewn, that *Impudence* and *Immodesty* are not so contrary to the Duties of *Women*, as *Prophaneness* is contrary to the Duty of a *Clergyman* For if there is the same Contrariety, then it must be equally monstrous for Women to encourage a Number of Women in an immodest Way of Life, as for *Bishops* and *Priests* to encourage a Number of Clergymen in a State of *Prophaneness*

Let us now take one Step farther in this Entertainment. The *Stage* has now upon it, *Venus, Bacchus, Silenus, Pan, Satyrs, Fawns, Sylvans, Bacchanals,* and *Bacchantes* Now if there were really such Beings as these, one would not wonder to see them got together As they have all one common Nature of *Vileness,* they are sufficiently recommended to one another But is it not astonishing, that these *fictitious Beings,* which are only imaginary Representations of such *Lust, Sensuality* and *Madness,* as never had any real Existence, but were invented by the Devil for the Delusion of the Heathen World, should be preserv'd to talk their filthy Language to Congregations of *Christians*! And perhaps *Silenus* never so publickly recommended *Lust* and *Impudence* in any Heathen Assembly, as he does here amongst Christians. For our

Stage

Stage has made him a fine Singer, that his Lewdness may have all the Recommendation, which a merry, strong Voice can give it.

Silenus   *Tho' envious old Age seems in part to impair me,*
                And make me the Sport of the Wanton and Gay;
                Brisk Wine shall recruit, as Life's Winter shall wear me;
                And I still have a Heart to do what I may
                Then, Venus, *bestow me some Dam'sel of Beauty;*
                Here's Bacchus *will furnish the cherishing Glass,*
                Silenus, *tho' grey, shall to both do his Duty;*
                And now clasp the Bottle, and then clasp the Lass

Surely no one will now think that I carry'd the Charge too high, when I call'd the *Play-House* the House of the *Devil*, for if his *fictitious Beings*, talking his Language, and acting such Parts as these, be not a sufficient Proof that it is his Work that is here carrying on, it is in vain to pretend to prove any thing. There is no Certainty that two and two are four.

If our Eyes could shew us the *holy Angels* in our Church-Assemblies, it would not be a stronger Proof of the Divine Presence, than the seeing such Images as these, and the hearing such Language from them, is a Proof that the *Stage* is the Devil's Ground   For how can he more certainly assure us of his Presence in any Place, than by *Satyrs, Bacchanals, Bacchantes,* and such like Images of Lewdness? He cannot appear to us as a Spirit, he must therefore get such *Beings* as *these* to appear for him, or, what seems to be more to his Purpose, make deluded Christians supply their Places   If therefore there be any certain Marks of the Devil's Power or Presence in any Assemblies, Places, or Temples of the Heathen World, the same are as certain Marks of his Power and Presence in our *Play-House.*

Again, Is it any Argument that the *Church* is God's House, because we there meet the *Ministers* of God, who act in his Name, because we there sing divine Hymns, hear holy Instructions, and raise our Hearts unto God and heavenly Matters, is this any Proof that we are then drawn near to God? If therefore there be a Place set apart for *lewd* and *prophane* Discourses, where the same Beings are introduc'd as filled Heathen Temples, where we celebrate their Power, and praise their Being with wanton Songs and impure Rant, and where we open our Hearts to the Impressions of wild and
dis-

diforder'd Paffions, is not this as certain a Proof, that fuch a *Place* muft belong to fome Being that is *contrary* to God, and that we are then as certainly drawn near to him? He that does not fee this with a fufficient Clearnefs, could never have feen that the Devil had any Power or Worfhip in the Heathen World You muft therefore obferve, that the *Play-Houfe* is not call'd the Houfe of the Devil only by way of Terror, and to fright you from a bad Place, but it is called fo, becaufe it really is fo in the ftricteft, fulleft Senfe of the Words

Let us now fuppofe, that the Diforders of the Stage cannot drive you from it; and that you are no more offended at the Meeting of thefe filthy Dæmons of the Heathen World, than if you was to meet your Friends

If this be your Cafe, how will you prove that your Religion has had any Effect upon you? Or that it has done you the leaft good? For if the fame Lewdnefs and Immorality pleafes you, which pleafed the Worfhippers of *Venus*; if you delight in fuch *Rant* and *Madnefs*, as was the Delight of *Bacchanals* and *Bacchantes*, is not this a Proof that you have the fame *Heart* and *Temper* that they had? And if you are like Idolaters in that which conftituted their Idolatry, have you any Reafon to think that Chriftianity has had any Effect upon you? It would even be *Prophanenefs* in any one to pretend to the true Spirit of Chriftianity, fo long as he can take pleafure in fuch an Entertainment as this For what is there that is unlike to the Spirit of Chrift, if this is not? Who that can rejoyce in the Lewdnefs and Beftiality of a *Silenus*, and the impure Rant of vile Dæmons, can make any Pretences to a reafonable Piety? Does this Company look as if we had any thing holy and divine in our Tempers? Is this living in the Spirit of Chrift? Is this the way to be as the Angels of God when we dye? Shall we go from the Pleafures of *Bacchus*, *Silenus*, *Bacchanals* and *Bacchantes*, to the Choir of bleffed Spirits that are above? Is there any Reafonablenefs or Fitnefs in thefe things? Why fhould we think, that fuch a Life as this will have an End fo contrary to it?

We reckon it ftrange Grofsnefs of Mind in the *Turks*, to expect a *Paradife* of carnal Delights But what a Degree of Grofsnefs is it in us, to know the God of Purity, and hope for a Heaven which only the *pure in Heart* fhall enjoy, and yet call up all the vile Fictions of Luft and Senfuality, that corrupted the Heathen World, to entertain our Hearts? That from their Mouths we may hear the Praifes of Debauchery

E and

and Wantonneſs? Let any one but conſider this, as every thing ought to be conſidered, by the pure Light of Reaſon and Religion, and he will find that the Uſe of the Stage may be reckon'd amongſt our worſt Sins, and that it is as great a Contradiction to our Religion, as any Corruption or vile Practice of the Heathen World

I have made theſe few Reflexions upon this Entertainment, not becauſe it exceeds the ordinary Wickedneſs of the Stage, but for the contrary Reaſon, becauſe it is far ſhort of it, and is much leſs offenſive than moſt of our *Plays.* That by ſhewing the *Stage* to be ſo impious and deteſtable, ſo contradictory to all Chriſtian Piety, in an Entertainment that is moderate, if compared with almoſt all our Plays, there might be no room left for ſober Chriſtians to be at any Peace with it. They who would ſee how much the Impieties of the Stage exceed what I have here obſerv'd of this Entertainment, may conſult Mr *Collier's* ſhort View of the Stage, Sir *Richard Blackmore's* Eſſays, and a *ſerious Remonſtrance,* &c. by Mr *Bedford.*

To return. *Levis* hears all theſe Arguments againſt the *Stage;* he owns they are very plain, and ſtrictly prove all that they pretend to, he does not offer one word againſt them, but ſtill *Levis* has an Anſwer for them *all,* without anſwering any *one* of them. I have, ſays he, my own Experience, that theſe Diverſions never did me any hurt, and therefore I ſhall uſe them.

But *Levis* does not conſider, that this very Anſwer ſhews, that he is very much hurt by them, that they have ſo much diſorder'd his Underſtanding, that he will defend his Uſe of them in the moſt abſurd manner imaginable, rather than be driven from them by any Arguments from Religion. For how can a Man ſhew that he is more hurt by any Practice, or that it has more blinded and perverted his Mind, than by appealing to his own inward Experience in Defenſe of it, againſt the plain Nature and Reaſon of things? Let *Levis* look at this way of reaſoning in other Matters. If a Perſon that prays in an *unknown Tongue,* ſhould diſregard all the Arguments that are brought to ſhew the Abſurdity of it, and reſt contented with ſaying, that it never hurt his Devotion, but that he was as much affected in that way, as he could poſſibly be in any other: *Levis* would certainly tell ſuch a one, that he had loſt his Underſtanding, and that his long Uſe

Use of such absurd Devotions, made him talk so absurdly about them.

Again. If a Worshipper of *Images* was, in Answer to the Second Commandment, only to say, that he had his own Experience that he found no hurt by them, and that he had the same Devotion of Heart to God, as if he did not worship *Images*. Or, suppose another Person to keep very ill Company, and when he is told, that *evil communications corrupt good manners*, should content himself with saying, that he would still use the same ill Company, because he was sure it did him no hurt, nor made any Impression upon him. Now as *Levis* would be sure that a Man was notoriously hurt by the Worship of *Images*, that should thus blindly defend them, and that the other is sufficiently hurt by ill Company, who should so obstinately stick to it, so he ought to be as sure, that he himself is sufficiently hurt either by Plays, or something else, when with an equal Blindness he defends his Use of them.

Farther. When *Levis* says, that he is sure that the Use of Plays does him no harm; let him consider, what he means by that Speech. Does he mean, that tho' he uses the Diversion of the Stage, yet he finds himself in the true State of Religion, that he has all those holy Tempers in that degree of Perfection which Christianity requireth? Now, if he cannot say this, how can he say, he is sure that Plays do him no harm? If a Person was to affirm, that Intemperance did him no hurt, it would be expected, that he should own that he was in a perfect State of Health. For, if he had any Disorder, or ill Habit of Body, he could not say, that his Intemperance did not contribute towards it. In like manner, if *Levis* will maintain, that Plays do no ways disorder him, or corrupt his Heart, he must affirm, that he has no Disorder or Corruption of Heart belonging to him; for if he has, he cannot say, that his Use of Plays does not contribute towards it.

When therefore *Levis* says, Plays do me no harm at all; it is the same thing as if he had said, I have no Disorder at all upon me; My Heart, and all my Tempers, are in that exact State of Purity and Perfection that they should be.

Again. Let *Levis* consider, that his Taste and Relish of the Stage, is a Demonstration that he is already hurt by something or other, and that his Heart is not in a right State of Religion. *Levis* thinks this is a very censorious Accusation; because he is known to be a very good Churchman, to live

a regua regular Life for the moſt part, to be charitable, and a Well-wiſher to all good Deſigns: All this is true of *Lewis* But then it is as ſtrictly true, that his Taſte for Plays is a Demonſtration, that his Heart is not in a right State of Religion. For, does *Lewis* think, that his frequenting the Church is any Sign of the State of his Heart? Am I to believe, that he has inward Diſpoſitions, that ſuit with the holy Strains of Divine Service, becauſe he likes to be at Church? I grant, I am to believe this; there is good Reaſon for it But then, if *Lewis* uſes the *Play-Houſe*, if the diſorder'd Paſſions, the lewd Images, the profane Rant, and immodeſt Parts that are there acted, are a Pleaſure to him, is not this as ſtrong a Demonſtration, that he has ſome Diſpoſitions and Tempers, that ſuit with theſe Diſorders? If I am to conclude any thing from a Man's liking and frequenting Divine Service, is there not as certain a Concluſion to be drawn from a Man's liking and uſing the Stage? For the Stage can no more be lik'd, without having ſome inward Corruptions that are ſuitable to the Diſorders that are there repreſented, than the Divine Service can be a Pleaſure to any one, that has no Holineſs or Devotion in his Heart

It is infallibly certain, that all Pleaſures ſhew the *State* and *Condition* of our Minds, and that nothing can pleaſe us, but what ſuits with ſome Diſpoſitions and Tempers that are within us; ſo that when we ſee a Man's Pleaſures, we are ſure that we ſee a great deal of his Nature All *Forms* of Life, all *outward* Actions may deceive us We can't abſolutely ſay, that People have ſuch Tempers, becauſe they do ſuch Actions, but where-ever People place any *Delight*, or receive any *Pleaſures*, there we have an infallible Token of ſomething in their Nature, and of what Tempers they have within them

Diverſions therefore, and Pleaſures, which are reckon'd ſuch uncertain Means of judging of the *State* of Men's Minds, are of all Means the moſt certain, becauſe nothing can pleaſe us, or affect us, but what is according to our Nature, and finds ſomething ⲧ ᵗhin us that is ſuitable to it Had we not inward Diſpoſitions of *Tenderneſs* and *Compaſſion*, we ſhould not find our ſelves ſoften'd and mov'd with *miſerable* Objects. Had we not ſomething *harmonious* in our Nature, we ſhould not find our ſelves pleas'd with Strains of *Muſick* In like manmer, had we not in our Nature lively Seeds of all thoſe Diſorders which are acted upon the Stage, were there not ſome

inward

inward Corruption, that finds it self gratify'd by all the irregular Paffions that are there reprefented, we fhould find no more Pleafure in the Stage, than blind Men find in *Pictures*, or deaf Men in *Mufick*

And, on the other fide, if we were full of the contrary Tempers, were our Hearts full of Affections contrary to thofe on the *Stage*, were we deeply affected with defires of Purity and Holinefs, we fhould find our felves as much offended with all that paffes upon the Stage, as *mild* and *gentle* Natures are offended at the fight of *Cruelty* and *Barbarity*. Thefe Things are of the utmoft Certainty

All People therefore who ufe the *Stage*, have as much Affurance that their Heart is not in a right State of Religion, as they poffibly can have of any Thing that relates to themfelves.

I hope, none of my Readers will think this too general, or too rafh an Affertion, but that they will rather obferve, that it is founded on fuch Evidence of Reafon, as cannot be rejected, without rejecting every Thing that is plain and certain in Human Nature They muft not think it a fufficient Anfwer to this, to confider either how good they are themfelves, or how many excellent Perfons they know, who do not abftain from the Stage For this is a way of reafoning, that is not allow'd in any other Cafe

Now, when it is affirm'd that all Perfons who are pleas'd with the *Stage*, muft have fome Corruptions of Heart, that are gratify'd with the corrupt Paffions which are there acted ; is not this as plain and evident, as if it were faid, that all who are pleas'd with feeing barbarous Actions, muft have fome Seeds of Barbarity in their Nature? If you are delighted with the Stroke of the *Whip*, and love to fee the *Blood* fly, is it not paft all doubt, that you have a Barbarity within you? And if *impure* Speeches, if *wanton* Amours, if *wild* Paffions, and *immoral* Rant, can give you any Delight, is it not equally paft all doubt, that you have fomething of all thefe Diforders in your Nature ? Is it any more uncharitable to affirm this, than to affirm, that all who love to fee the *Blood* fly, have fomething barbarous in their Nature ? Is there any more Rafhnefs or Severity in it, than in faying, that all who love fuch or fuch Strains of *Mufick*, have fome Difpofition in their Nature, that is gratified by them ?

It fignifies nothing therefore to fay, that you know fuch or fuch excellent Perfons who are pleas'd with the *Stage*, whom no one ought to fufpect to be defective in Piety, it is as ab-

furd

furd as to fay, that you know excellent Perfons who are pleas'd with feeing barbarous Actions, whom no one ought to fufpect to be defective in *Tenderness*. If you delight in barbarous Sights, and are pleas'd with the Groans and Pains of the Afflicted, I don't *fufpect* you to be defective in *Tenderness*, you have put your Cafe out of all Sufpicion, you have prov'd that you have a Barbarity in your Nature. So if you delight in the *Stage*, if you tafte and relifh its Entertainment, I don't *fufpect* you to be *defective* in Piety; you have put your Cafe beyond Sufpicion; you have prov'd that you have Difpofitions in your Nature, that are gratify'd by the diforderly Paffions of the *Stage*

Again, confider it in another View: How is it poffible that any one fhould delight in the *Stage*, but thro' a Defect in Piety? For is not the Stage guilty of Impurity, Prophanenefs, Blafphemy, and Immorality? Now tho' People may differ about the Degree in which they will make this Charge, yet all muft own it in fome degree. Now if the Charge be but true in *any degree*, muft there not be a Want of Piety in thofe that can partake of an Entertainment chargeable with *Impurity*, *Prophanenefs*, and *Immorality*? If People were fo pious that they could not bear fuch an Entertainment as this; if nothing could perfuade them to be prefent at it, this would be no Proof that they were Saints, for to abhor an Entertainment loaded with fo much Guilt, is but a fmall Inftance of an advanc'd Piety. But furely, if they can not only bear it, but be pleas'd with it, it is Proof enough that their Hearts want feveral Degrees of Piety, which become Chriftians. Befides, can pious Perfons, who ufe the *Stage*, tell you of any *one Play* for this forty ❦ fifty Years, that has been free from *wild* Rant, *immodeft* Paffions, and *prophane* Language? Muft they not therefore be defective in Piety, who partake of a Diverfion that is at *no time* free from this Guilt in fome degree or other? But fuppofing there were fuch a thing as an *innocent Play* once or twice in an Age, (which is like fuppofing *innocent* Luft, *fober* Rant, or harmlefs Prophanenefs) could this make it at all allowable for pious Perfons to ufe the *Stage*? Could this be any Proof that Perfons of real Piety might take pleafure in it? For could it be confiftent with an enliven'd Piety to ufe a Diverfion, which in its *common ordinary* State is full of monftrous Impiety and Prophanenefs, becaufe it fometimes happen'd in a Number of Years, that it might be innocent for a *Day* or *two*? But even this does not happen. The Stage never has *one* innocent Play, not one

one can be produced that ever you faw acted in *either Houfe*, but what abounds with *Thoughts*, *Paffions* and *Language* contrary to Religion. Is there therefore any Rafhnefs or Severity in faying, That Perfons who ufe a Diverfion, which in its *ordinary* State is full of monftrous Wickednefs and Impiety, and in its *beft* State never free from Variety of Sin, to fay that fuch Perfons muft be defective in Piety? How can we know any thing with Clearnefs and Evidence, if we don't know this to be clear and evident? For furely it is a neceffary Part of Piety to abhor Lewdnefs, Immorality, or Prophanenefs, where-ever they are, but they who are fo pious as not to be able to be pleas'd where any of thofe are, have a Piety that will not permit them ever to fee a Play

There is no Doctrine of our Bleffed Saviour, that more concerns all Chriftians, or is more effential to their Salvation than this· *Bleffed are the pure in heart, for they fhall fee God* Now take the *Stage* in its beft State, when fome admir'd *Tragedy* is upon it, are the *extravagant Paffions* of diftracted Lovers, the *impure Ravings* of inflam'd Heroes, the *Joys* and *Torments* of Love, and *grofs Defcriptions* of Luft; are the *indecent* Actions, the *amorous* Tranfports, the *wanton Addrefs* of the Actors, which make fo great a Part of the *moft fober* and *modeft* Tragedies, are thefe things confiftent with this Chriftian Doctrine of *Purity of Heart?* You may as well imagine, that *Murder* and *Rapine* are confiftent with *Charity* and *Meeknefs*.

It is therefore as neceffary, as reafonable, and as confiftent with Chriftian Charity, to tell *Levis*, that his Ufe and Delight in the *Stage* is a certain Proof of his want of Piety, as to tell the fame thing to a malicious, intemperate, or revengeful Perfon Some People who are guilty of perfonal Vices may have fome Violence of Temptation, fome natural Diforder to plead in their Excufe; they perhaps may be fo tender as to defire to conceal them, and be afraid to encourage others in the like Practices; but the Ufe and Encouragement of the *Stage* has no Excufes of this kind, it has no *Infirmity*, *Surprize*, or *Violence* of Temptation to appeal to; it fhews no *Tendernefs* of Mind, or *Concern* for others, but is a deliberate, continued, open and publick Declaration in favour of *Lewdnefs*, *Immorality* and *Prophanenefs*. Let any one but collect, not all the Wickednefs that has appear'd on the Stage fince he firft ufed it, but only fo much as paffes there in *any one* Seafon, and then he will fee what a dreadful Load of Guilt he has brought upon himfelf. For furely no one can be fo
weak

weak as to imagine, that he can use and encourage a wicked Entertainment, without making himself a *full Sharer* of all its Wickedness

Archbishop *Tillotson* treats the Stage in this manner. ' I ' shall now speak a few Words concerning *Plays*, which as ' they are now order'd amongst us, are a *mighty Reproach* to ' the Age and Nation ------As now the Stage is, they are ' *intolerable*, and not fit to be permitted in a *civiliz'd*, much ' less a *Christian* Nation They do most *notoriously* minister ' to Infidelity and Vice -----And therefore I do not see how ' any Person *pretending* to Sobriety and Virtue, and especially ' to the *pure* and *holy* Religion of our Blessed Saviour, can ' without *great Guilt*, and open *Contradiction* to his holy Pro- ' fession, be present at such lewd and immodest Plays, as too ' many do, who yet would take it very ill to be shut out of ' the Community of Christians, as they would most cer- ' tainly have been in the first and purest Ages of Christia- ' nity *

Here let it be observ'd, that this Archbishop, who has ge- nerally been reckon'd eminent for his *Moderation* and *gentle* manner of treating every thing, says of Plays, that they are a *mighty Reproach* to the Nation, that they are *intolerable*, and not fit to be permitted in a *Civiliz'd*, much less a *Christian Nation*, that they *notoriously* minister to *Infidelity* and *Vice*

Now this, I suppose, is as high a Charge, as he would have brought against the worst Articles of *Popery* If I have said, that People cannot use the *Stage* without being defective in Piety, I have not said it in a declaiming way, but have as- serted it from Variety of plain Arguments But this great Man, so much admired for his *tender* Remarks upon *Persons* and *Things*, goes much farther He does not say, that People of real and advanc'd Piety cannot use the *Stage*, but he makes it inconsistent with so much as *pretending to Sobriety and Vir- tue*, much less the *Purity* and *holy Religion* of our blessed Sa- viour. He does not say, that such People cannot be Excel- lent and Exemplary Christians, or that they must be defective in Piety, but he charges them with *great Guilt*, and *open Con- tradiction* to their Holy Religion, and assures them, that if they had liv'd in the *first* and *purest* Ages of Christianity, they would have been excommunicated.

---

* *Serm upon corrupt Communication.*

I have

I have appeal'd to this *great Name*, for no other End, but to prevent the Charge of Uncharitableness. For surely, if such an eminent Instance of a *charitable* and *gentle* Spirit can roundly affirm, that the Use of such a *Stage* as ours is an *open Contradiction* to Christianity, and such a scandalous Offence, as would certainly have been punish'd in the first and purest Ages of the Church, by the dreadful Punishment of Excommunication, surely it can be no Proof of an *uncharitable Spirit* in me, that I shew by Variety of Arguments, that the Use of such a *Stage* cannot consist with the true Spirit of Christianity, but that there must be *some Defect* in their Piety, who are able to use it.

Jucunda resolves in great Chearfulness to hear no Arguments against the *Stage*. She says it can be but a *small Sin*, and, considering the Wickedness of the Age, that Person is in a very good State, that is only guilty of going to Plays. Desire her ever so often only to consider the plainest Argument in the World, she puts all off with only this Reply, *God send I may have no greater Sin to answer for, than seeing a Play!*
Jucunda thinks a Clergyman would do better, to insist only upon the Material Parts of Religion, and not put so much Stress upon Things that are only *Diversions*, lest by making Religion to contradict People in every thing, Religion it self should be brought into dislike. *Jucunda* desires, that she may be instructed in some greater Things, than the Sinfulness of going to a *Play*, for she is resolved to hear no more of that.
But pray, *Jucunda*, consider all that you have here said. You say, it can be but a *small Sin*. How is it that you know it is but a *small Sin*? What care have you taken to understand its true Magnitude? You shut your Eyes, and stop your Ears, and resolve against all Information about it, and then call it a *small Sin*. But suppose it were but a *small Sin*, is that a Reason why you should be guilty of it? Does the Smalness of Sins recommend them to your Choice? Our blessed Saviour saith, * *If thy foot offend thee, cut it off, it is better for thee to enter halt into life, than having two feet, to be cast into hell. And if thine eye offend thee, pluck it out;*

---

* Mark ix. 47.

F

it is better for thee to enter into the kingdom of God with one eye, than having two eyes, to be cast into hell-fire Now this passage, I suppose, does not mean, If thou art guilty of some great Sin, either of *Murder*, *Perjury*, or the like, thou must cut them off For, the Comparison of a *Foot* and an *Eye*, must signify something that is not directly sinful in it self, but only dangerous in its *Use*, as it sets us too near to some Sins, or is become too full of Temptation Yet such ways of Life as these, which are only dangerous, and expose our Virtue to too great a Hazard, however pleasant and useful, (tho' like an *Eye*, or *Foot*) are yet to be entirely cut off, that we may not fall into Hell-fire Can it be suppos'd that *Jucunda* is of this Religion, who pleases her self with a Diversion, because it is but a *small Sin*? Will she ever think of saving her self, by cutting off a *Foot*, or plucking out an *Eye*?

Indeed, to talk of a *small Sin*, is like talking of a *small Law* of God. For, as there is no Law of God, but is a great one, because it comes from God; so every Sin, as it is a Transgression of some Law of God, must needs be a great one. There may be Sins that have a smaller degree of Guilt, because they may be committed thro' *Infirmity*, *Ignorance*, or *Surprize*, but no Sin is small, that is either carelesly or wilfully continued in If it be a Sin therefore to use the *Stage*, it cannot be a *small one*, because it has none of those Circumstances which render a Sin a small one It becomes a very great one to *Jucunda*, because she carelesly and wilfully resolves to continue in it, merely for the sake of a little Diversion

Let *Jucunda* consider again, what she means by wishing that she may have no greater Sin to answer for than going to a Play It is a Wish that is silly in itself, because she is not to wish to dye in small Sins, but in a perfect Repentance and Abhorrence of all kind of Sin, but it is much sillier still, when it is given as a Reason for going to a *Play*. For it is saying, *I expect to dye guilty of greater Sins than of going to a Play, and therefore there is no Occasion to forbear from that* Now if she understands herself she must know, that this is the plain Meaning of her Words Yet who that understands any thing of Religion, or that has any Desire of Holiness can talk at this rate? It is a Language that is fitter for an *Atheist*, than for a Person that is but *half* a Christian. If a Tradesman that allows himself only to lye in the Prices of his Goods, should content himself with saying, *God send I may have*

have no greater Sins to answer for, no one would suppose him to be much concern'd about Religion. Yet as many Christian Reasons might be produced to shew these Lies to be but small Sins, as to shew that the Use of the Stage is but a *small Sin*.

Jucunda would have a *Clergyman* insist upon the most material Parts of Religion, and not lay so much stress upon things that are only *Diversions*. I am of your mind, *Jucunda*, that a Clergyman ought to insist upon the most material Parts of Religion, but then it does not follow, that he must not lay much stress upon things that are *Diversions*. For as something that is called a Diversion may be entirely sinful, so if this should happen, it is as necessary for a Clergyman to call all Christians from it, as it is necessary to exhort them to keep the Commandments. Religion seems to have as little to do with *Trades*, as with *Diversions*, yet if a Trade be set up, that is in its own Nature wicked, there is nothing more material in Religion, than to declare the Necessity of forsaking such an Employment. But after all, *Jucunda*, the most essential, and most *material* Parts of Religion are such as relate to *common Life*, such as alter our Ways of living, such as give Rules to all our Actions, and are the Measure of all our Conduct, whether in Business or Diversion. Nothing is so important in Religion to you, as that which makes you sober and wise, holy and heavenly-minded in the whole Course of your Life. But you are for such *material Parts* of Religion, as should only distinguish you from a *Jew* or an *Infidel*, but make no Difference in common Life betwixt you and *Fops* and *Coquets*. You are for a Religion that consists in Modes and Forms of Worship, that is ty'd to *Times* and *Places*, that only takes up a little of your time on *Sunday*, and leaves you all the Week to do as you please. But all this, *Jucunda*, is nothing. The Scripture hath not said in vain, *He that is in Christ is a new Creature*. All the Law and the Gospel are in vain to you; all Sacraments, Devotions, Doctrines and Ordinances are to no purpose, unless they make you this *new Creature* in all the Actions of your Life. He teaches you the most material Parts of Religion, who teaches you to be of a *religious Spirit* in every thing that you do, who teaches you to eat and drink, to labour and rest, to converse and divert yourself in such degrees, and to such Ends, as best promote a pious Life.

If *Sots* and *Gluttons* should desire a *Clergyman* to insist upon the most material Parts of Religion, and not lay so great

a stress

a ftrefs upon *Gluttony* and *Intemperance*, which are things that only relate to *eating* and *drinking*, they would fhew that they underftood Religion as well as *Jucunda* For every one muft fee, that *fome Diverfions* may as much diforder the Heart, and be as contrary to Religion, as *Gluttony* and *Intemperance* And perhaps as many People have liv'd and dy'd unaffected with Religion, thro' a Courfe of *Diverfions* and *Pleafures*, as thro' Gluttony and Intemperance

If it difpleafes People to be told, that Religion is to prefcribe Rules to their Diverfions, they are as unreafonable as thofe are, who are difpleas'd that Religion fhould prefcribe Rules to their Tempers, and Paffions, and Inclinations For as Diverfions are only the Gratifications of our Tempers, fo if Religion is to forbear us in our Diverfions, it is to forbear our Tempers, Paffions and Inclinations But the Truth is, we ought to be more religioufly cautious and watchful about our Diverfions, than any other Part of common Life, not only becaufe they take fuch deep hold of us, but becaufe they have no neceffary Foundation in Nature, but are our own Inventions *Trade* and Bufirefs, tho' they are neceffary for great Ends of Life, are yet to be fubject to the ftricteft Rules of Religion, furely therefore *Diverfions*, which are but like fo many *Blanks* in Life, that are only invented to get rid of Time, furely fuch things ought of all others to have no *mixture* of any thing that is finful in them For if the thing it felf be hardly pardonable, furely it muft be a high Crime to add to it the Sin of doing it in a finful manner For as Diverfions are at beft only Methods of lofing Time, the moft innocent have fomething in them that feems to want a Pardon, but if we cannot be content with fuch as only pafs away our Hours, unlefs they gratify our diforder'd Paffions, we are like thofe who are not content to fleep away their time, unlefs they can add the Pleafure of finful Dreams ·

Jucunda therefore is much miftaken, if fhe thinks that Religion has nothing to do with her Diverfions, for there is nothing that requires a more religious Exactnefs than they do. If we are wrong in them, it is the fame thing as if we are wrong in our Religion, or finful in our Bufinefs Nay, Sin in our Diverfions is lefs excufable, and perhaps does us more harm than in any thing elfe For fuch as our Diverfions are, fuch are we our felves If Religion therefore is to have any Power over us, if it is to enter into our Hearts, and alter and reform the State of our Souls, the greateft Work that it has

to

to do, is to remove us from such Pleasures and Ways of Life, as nourish and support a wrong State of our Souls

If dying Sinners that go out of the World under a Load of Guilt could see what brought them into that State, it would often be found, that all their Sins, and Impieties, and Neglects of Duty, were solely owing to their Diversions; and perhaps were they to live their Lives over again, there would be no other possible way of living better than they had done, but by renouncing such ways of Life, as were only look'd upon as Diversions and Amusements

People of Fashion and Quality have great Advantage above the Vulgar; their Condition and Education gives them a Liveliness and Brightness of Parts, from whence one might justly expect a more exalted Virtue   How comes it then, that we see as ill *Morals*, as open *Impiety*, as little *religious Wisdom*, and as great *Disorders* among them, as among the most rude, uneducated Part of the World ? It is because the *Politeness* of their Lives, their Course of Diversions and Amusements, and their Ways of spending their time, as much extinguishes the *Wisdom* and *Light* of Religion, as the Grossness and Ignorance of the dullest Part of the World   A poor Creature that is doom'd to a stupid Conversation, that sees nothing but *Drudgery*, and *Eating*, *Drinking* and *Sleeping*, is as likely to have his Soul aspire to God, and aim at an exalted Virtue, as another that is always in the Brightness and Gayety of polite Pleasures   It is the same thing whether the *good Seed* be burnt up with the Heat and Brightness of the *Sun*, or be lost in *Mud*   Many Persons that live and dye in a *Mine*, that are confin'd to Drudgery and Darkness, are just so fatally destroy'd by their way of Life, as others that live in a Circle of Pleasures and polite Engagements are destroy'd by their way of Life.   Every one sees and owns the Effects of such a gross way of Life, it is not usual to expect any thing wise, or holy, or truly great, from Persons that live and dye digging *Coals*   But then it is not enough consider'd, that there are other Ways of Life of a contrary Appearance, that as certainly and unavoidably produce the same Effects. For a Heart that is devoted to *polite* Pleasures, that is taken up with a Succession of vain and corrupt *Diversions*, that is employ'd in *Assemblies*, *Gaming*, *Plays*, *Balls*, and such like Business of a *genteel* Life, is as much dispos'd of, and taken as far out of the way of true Religion, and a divine and holy Life, as if it had been shut up in a *Mine*   These are plain and certain Truths, if there is any thing plain and cer-

tain,

tain, either in the Nature of Religion, or the Nature of Man. Who expects Piety from a *Tapster*, that lives amongst the Rudeness, Noise and Intemperance of an *Alehouse*? Who expects Christian Holiness from a *Juggler*, that goes about with his *Cups* and *Balls*? Yet why is not this as reasonable, as to expect Piety and Christian Holiness from a *fine Gentleman* that lives at a *Gaming-Table*? Is there any more reason to look for Christian Fortitude, divine Tempers, or religious Greatness of Mind in this State of Life? Had such a one been born in low Life with the same turn of Mind, it had in all probability fix'd him in an *Ale-house*, or furnish'd him with *Cups* and *Balls*.

The sober, honest Employments of Life, and the reasonable Cares of every Condition in the World, makes it sufficiently difficult for People to live enough to God, and to act with such holy and wise Tempers as Religion requireth. But if we make our Wealth and Fortunes the Gratifications of idle and disorder'd Passions, we may make it as difficult to be saved in a State of *Politeness* and *Genteelity*, as in the *basest* Occupations of Life.

Religion requires a steady, resolute Use of our best Reason, and an earnest Application to God for the Light and Assistance of his Holy Spirit.

It is only this watchful Temper, that is full of Attention to every thing that is right and good, that watches over our Minds, and guards our Hearts, that loves Reason, that desires Wisdom, and constantly calls upon God for the Light and Joy of his holy Spirit; it is this Temper alone that can preserve us in any true State of Christian Holiness. There is no Possibility of having our Minds strengthen'd and fix'd in wise and reasonable Judgments, or our Hearts full of good and regular Motions, but by living in such a *way of Life*, as assists and improves our Reason, and prepares and disposes us to receive the Spirit of God. This is as certainly the *one only* way to Holiness, as there is but one God that is Holy. Religion can no more subsist in a trifling, vain Spirit, that lives by Humour and Fancy, that is full of Levity and Impertinence, wandring from Passion to Passion, giddy with silly Joys, and burden'd with impertinent Cares, it can no more subsist with this State of the Soul, than it can dwell in a Heart *devoted* to Sin.

Any way of Life therefore that darkens our Minds, that misemploys our Reason, that fills us with a trifling Spirit, that disorders our Passions, that separates us from the Spirit of God,

God, is the same certain Road to Destruction; whether it arise from stupid *Sensuality*, rude *Ignorance*, or polite *Pleasures*. Had any one therefore the Power of an *Apostle*, or the Tongue of an *Angel*, he could not employ it better, than in censuring and condemning those ways of Life, which *Wealth*, *Corruption*, and *Politeness* have brought amongst us. We, indeed, only call them Diversions, but they do the whole Work of *Idolatry* and *Infidelity*, and fill People with so much Blindness and Hardness of Heart, that they neither live by Reason, nor feel the want of it, but are content to play away their Lives, as regardless of every Thing that is wise, and holy, and divine, as if they were mere *Birds*, or *Animals*, and as thoughtless of Death, and Judgment, and Eternity, as if these were Things that had no Relation to human Life

Now, all this Blindness and Hardness of Heart is owing to that way of Life, which People of Fortune generally fall into It is not gross Sins, it is not *Murder*, or *Adultery*, but it is their *Genteelity* and *Politeness*, that destroys them It fills them with such Passions and Pleasures, as quite extinguish the gentle Light of Reason and Religion For, if Religion requireth a sober Turn of Mind, if we cannot be reasonable, but by subduing and governing our blind Tempers and Passions, if the most necessary Enjoyments of Life require great Caution and Sobriety, that our Souls be not made earthly and sensual by them; what way of Life can so waste and destroy our Souls, what can so strengthen our Passions, and disorder our Hearts, as a Life of such Diversions, Entertainments and Pleasures, as are the *Business* of great Part of the World?

If Religion is to reform our Souls, to deliver us from the Corruption of our Nature, to restore the divine Image, and fill us with such Tempers of Purity and Perfection, as may fit us for the Eternal Enjoyment of God, what is the polite Part of the World a doing? For how can any one more renounce such a Religion as this, how can he more resist the Grace of God, and hinder the Recovery of the Divine Image, than by living in a Succession of such Enjoyments, as the Generality of People of Fashion are devoted to? For no one, who uses the *Stage*, has any more Reason to expect to grow in the Grace of God, or to be enlighten'd and purify'd by his Holy Spirit, than he that never uses any Devotion. So that it is not to be wonder'd at, if the Spirit and Power of Religion is wanted, where People so live, as neither to be fit to receive, nor able to co-operate with the Affistance and Light of God's Holy Spirit

We are taught, that *Charity covereth the multitude of fins*; and, that *alms fhall purge away fins* Now, let this teach fome People how to judge of the Guilt of thofe Gifts and Contributions, which are given contrary to Charity I don't mean fuch Money, as is idly and impertinently fquander'd away; but fuch *Gifts* and *Contributions*, as are to fupport People in a wicked Life For, this is fo great a Contradiction to Charity, that it muft certainly have Effects contrary to it It muft as much cover our *Virtues*, as Charity covereth our *Sins*

It is no ftrange Thing, to hear of *Ladies* taking care of a *Benefit-Night* in the Play-Houfe But furely, they never reflect upon what they are doing For if there is any Bleffing that attends Charity, there muft as great a Curfe attend fuch Liberalities, as are to reward People for their Wickednefs, and make them happy and profperous in an unchriftian Profeffion How can they expect the Bleffings of God, or to have their Virtues and Charities placed to their Account, when they have blotted them out, by their Contributions and Generofities to the moft open Enemies of the Purity and Holinefs of Chrift's Religion? He that is thus with the Play-Houfe, is moft openly againft God, and is as certainly oppofing Religion, as he that rewards thofe that labour in the Caufe of Infidelity

It is no uncharitable Affertion, to affirm, that a Player cannot be a living Member of Chrift, or in a true State of Grace, till he renounces his Profeffion, with a fincere and deep Repentance Chriftianity no more allows fuch Plays and Players as ours are, than it allows the groffeft Vices They are Objects of no other Charity, or Kindnefs, than fuch as may reduce them to a fincere Repentance What a Guilt therefore do they bring upon themfelves, who make Players their Favourites, and publick Objects of their Care and Generofity, who cannot be in the Favour of God, till they ceafe to be fuch as they encourage them to be, till they renounce that Life, for which they efteem and reward them?

When an Object of *Diftrefs* is offer'd to People, it is common to fee them very fcrupulous in their Charity, they feem to think there may be fuch a thing as a blameable Charity; they defire to know whether the Perfon be worthy, whether his Diftrefs is not owing to his Follies and Extravagancies; that they may not relieve fuch a one, as ought to feel the

Punifh-

Punifhment of his Follies But what muft we fay to thefe things, if thofe who are thus nice in their *Alms*, are yet unreafonable in their *Generofities*, who are afraid of affifting a poor Man, till every thing can be faid in his Favour; and yet eager to make another rich, who is only recommended by his Follies? What fhall we fay to thefe things, if Perfons who have fo many Rules to govern and reftrain their Pity to poor Men, have yet no Rules to govern their Liberalities and Kindnefs to Libertines? If they fhall have a *Benefit-Night* upon their hands, not to relieve the Poverty, but to reward the *Merit* of a Player, that he may have the Subfiftence of a *Gentleman* from Chriftians, for a way of Life that would be a Reproach to a fober Heathen? Shall we reckon this amongft our fmall Offences? Is this a pardonable Inftance of the Weaknefs of human Nature? Is it not rather an undeniable Proof, that Chriftianity has no hold of our Reafon and Judgment? And that we muft be born again from fuch a State of Heart as this, before we can enter into the Spirit of Chriftianity?

I have now only one thing to defire of the Reader, Not that he would like and approve of thefe Reflexions, but that he will not fuffer himfelf to diflike or condemn them, till he has put his Arguments into Form, and knows how many Doctrines of Scripture he can bring againft thofe things that I have afferted So far as he can fhew that I have reafoned wrong, or miftook the Doctrine of Scripture, fo far he has a Right to cenfure But *general Diflikes* are mere *Tempers*, as blind as *Paffions*, and are always the ftrongeft where Reafons are moft wanted If People will diflike, becaufe they will, and condemn Doctrines, only becaufe it fuits better with their *Tempers* and *Practices*, than to confider and underftand them to be true, they act by the fame Spirit of *Popery*, as is moft remarkable in the *loweft Bigots*, who are refolute in a *general Diflike* of all *Proteftant* Doctrines, without fuffering themfelves to confider and underftand upon what Truth they are founded

I can eafily imagine, that fome People will cenfure thefe Doctrines, as proceeding from a *rigid, uncharitable* Temper, becaufe they feem to condemn fo great a Part of the World. Had I wrote a Treatife againft *Covetoufnefs* or *Intemperance*, it had certainly condemned great Part of the World, but furely he muft have ftrangely forgot himfelf, that fhould make that a Reafon of accufing me of an uncharitable Temper.

Such

Such People fhould confider alfo, that a Man cannot affert the Doctrines of Chriftian *Charity* and *Meeknefs* themfelves, without condemning a very great Part of the World. But would it be an Inftance of an uncharitable Spirit, to preach up the Neceffity of an univerfal Charity, becaufe it might condemn a very great Part of the World? And if the *Holinefs* of Chriftianity cannot be afferted, without condemning the Pleafures and Entertainments of the fafhionable Part of the World, is there any more Uncharitablenefs in this, than in afferting the Doctrine of univerfal Love? Does this any more fhew an *unchriftian, rigid* Spirit, than when the beloved Apoftle faid, *All that is in the World, the Luft of the Flefh, the Luft of the Eyes, and the Pride of Life, is not of the Father, but is of the World?*

But I fhall not now confider any more Objections, but leave all that I have faid to the Confcience and Reafon of every Perfon Let him but make Reafon and Religion the Meafure of his Judgment, and then he is as favourable to me as I defire him to be

It is very common and natural for People to ftruggle hard, and be loth to own any thing to be wrong that they have long practis'd Many People will fee fo much Truth in thefe Arguments againft the *Stage,* that they will wifh in their own Minds that they had always forbore it But then finding that they cannot affent to thefe Arguments without taking a great deal of blame to themfelves, they will find ftrong Inclinations to condemn the plaineft Reafonings, rather than condemn themfelves Let but a Perfon forget that he has any Guilt in relation to the *Stage,* let him but fuppofe that he has never been there, and that he will go or ftay away, juft as he finds Reafon, when he has examin'd all that can be faid againft it, let a Man but put himfelf in this State of Mind, and then he will fee all the Arguments againft the Stage, as plain and convincing, as any that can be brought againft the groffeft Vices

If we could look into the Minds of the feveral Sorts of Readers, we fhould fee how differently People are affected with Arguments, according to the State that they are in. We fhould fee how thofe, who have never ufed the *Stage,* confent with the whole Force of their Minds, and fee the Certainty and Plainnefs of every Argument againft it We fhould fee others ftruggling and contending againft all Conviction, in proportion to the Ufe that they have made of the *Stage* Thofe that have been its Friends and Advocates, and conftant Admirers, will hate the very Name of a Book that is wrote againſt it, and will condemn every Argument, without knowing what it is Thoſe who have uſed the *Stage* much, tho' in a leſs degree than this, will perhaps vouchſafe to read a Book againſt it, but they will read with Fear; they will ſtrive not to be convinced, and be angry at every Argument, for proving ſo much as it does. Others, that have uſed the *Stage* in the moſt moderate degree, have yet great Prejudices They perhaps will own, that the *Stage* is blameable, and that it is very well to perſwade People from it But then, theſe People will not aſſent to the whole Truth They will not condemn the Stage, as they ought, becauſe having been there ſometimes themſelves, it ſuits better with their own Practice only to condemn it in the general, than to declare it to be ſinful in ſuch a degree, as ſhould condemn thoſe who ever uſe it

These are the ſeveral Difficulties, which this Treatiſe has to contend with. It is to oppoſe an Evil Practice, and charge it with *ſuch a Degree* of Guilt, as few can conſent to, without taking ſome Part of that Guilt to themſelves.

I have mention'd theſe ſeveral Degrees of Prejudice, to put People upon ſuſpecting themſelves, and trying the State of their Hearts For, the only way to be wiſe and reaſonable, is to ſuſpect our ſelves, and put Queſtions to our ſelves in private, which only our own Hearts can anſwer. Let any one who reads this Treatiſe, aſk himſelf, whether he reads it, as he reads thoſe Things which have no Relation to himſelf? When he reads a Treatiſe againſt *Image-Worſhip*, or Prayers to *Saints*, he knows that he attends to the whole Force, of the Arguments, that he deſires to ſee them in their full Strength, and to comprehend every Evil that they charge upon it. Now every one can tell, whether he reads this Treatiſe with this Temper, or whether he comes heavily to it, and unwilling to be convinced by it. If this is his State, he ought to charge himſelf with all that, which he charges upon the moſt abſurd and perverſe People in Life For it is only this Temper, an *Inclination* not to be convinc'd, that makes People ſo *poſitive* and *obſtinate* in Ways and Opinions, that appear ſo ſhocking to all reaſonable Men It is this Temper, that makes the *Jew*, the *Infidel*, the *Papiſt* and the *Fanatick*, of every kind And he that is not reaſonable enough to read impartially a Treatiſe againſt the *Stage*, has no Reaſon to think, that his Mind is in better Order than theirs is, who cannot freely conſider a Book that is wrote againſt the *Worſhip of Images*, and Prayers to *Saints*

There

There is but one Thing for reasonable People to do in this Case, Either to answer all the Arguments here produced against the *Stage*, or to yield to the Truth of them, and regulate their Lives according to them Our Conduct in this Affair is far from being a small Matter. I have produced no Arguments, but such as are taken from the most Essential Parts of Religion If therefore there is any Truth in them, the Use of the *Stage* is certainly to be reckon'd amongst *great* and *flagrant* Sins.

I have now only to advise those, who are hereby made sensible of the Necessity of renouncing the *Stage*, that they will act in this Case, as they expect that others should act in Cases of the like nature That they will not think it sufficient to forbear the Stage themselves, but be instrumental as far as they can in keeping others from it, and that they will think it as necessary to make this amends for their former Compliance and ill Example, as it is necessary to make *Restitution* in cases of Injury The Cause of Religion, the Honour of God, the Good of their Neighbour, and the Peace and Satisfaction of their own Minds, necessarily requires this at their Hands For as no one can tell how far his Example may have influenc'd others, and how many People may have been injur'd by his means, so it is absolutely necessary, that he do as much good as he can, by a better Example, and make his own Change of Life a Means of reducing others to the same State of Amendment

F I N I S.

BOOKS Printed for W *and* J INNYS, *at the West End of St.* Paul's. 1726

1. A Practical Treatise upon Christian Perfection. By *William Law*, A. M 8*vo.* 1726

2. Mr. *Law*'s Remarks upon a late Book entituled, *The Fable of the Bees* or, *Private Vices Publick Benefits* In a Letter to the Author. To which is added, a Postscript, containing an Observation or two upon Mr. *Bayle.* The third Edition 8*vo.* 1726.

3. ——— His three Letters to the Bishop of *Bangor.* The eighth Edition. 8*vo.* 1721.

4. The Absolute Unlawfulness of the Stage Entertainment fully demonstrated By *William Law*, A. M. The second Edition. 8*vo.* 1726

5. A moral Proof of the Certainty of a Future State. 8*vo.* 1725.

6. Reasons against Conversion to the Church of *Rome.* In a Letter to his Guardian, a late Convert to that Church. By a Student of the *Temple* 8*vo.* 1726.

7. The true Meaning of the Fable of the Bees In a Letter to the Author of a Book entitled, An Enquiry whether a general Practice of Virtue tends to the Wealth or Poverty, Benefit or Disadvantage of a People? Shewing that he has manifestly mistaken the true Meaning of the Fable of the Bees in his Reflections on that Book. 8*vo.* 1726.

8. The Principles of Deism truly represented and set in a clear Light, in two Dialogues between a *Sceptick* and a *Deist.* The first concerning the Christian Revelation, the second concerning Natural Religion. The third Edition. 8*vo.* 1724

9. *The Christian Institutes*, or, *The sincere Word of God.* Being a plain and impartial Account of the whole Faith and Duty of a Christian, collected out of the Writings of the Old and New Testaments. Digested under proper Heads, and delivered in the Words of Scripture, by the Right Reverend Father in God, *Francis* Lord Bishop of *Chester.* The fourth Edition. 12*o.* 1721.

10. I cur-

10. Fourteen Difcourfes preached on feveral Occafions, by *William Shorey*, A. M. Lecturer of St. *Lawrence-Jewry*. 8*vo*. 1725.

11. Directions, Counfels and Cautions, tending to prudent Management of Affairs in common Life. Collected by *Thomas Fuller*, M. D. 12*o*. 1725.

12. An Addrefs to Parents, fhewing them the Obligations they are under to take care of the Chriftian Education of their Children, and laying before them the principal Points in which they ought to inftruct them. By *Jofeph Hoole*, Vicar of *Haxey*. 8*vo*. 1724.

13. Three Dialogues between *Hylas* and *Philonous*. The Defign of which is plainly to demonftrate the Reality and Perfections of human Knowledge, the incorporeal Nature of the Soul, and the immediate Providence of a Deity, in oppofition to Scepticks and Atheifts. Alfo to open a Method for rendring the Sciences more eafy, ufeful and compendious. By *George Berkley*, M. A. Fellow of *Trinity* College, *Dublin*. The fecond Edition 8*vo*. 1725.

14. Pious Thoughts concerning the Knowledge and Love of God, and other holy Exercifes. By the late Archbifhop of *Cambray*, together with a Letter of Chriftian Inftruction, by a Lady, done out of *French*. 8*vo* 1720.

15 A Difcourfe of the Truth and Certainty of Natural Religion, and the indifpenfible Obligations to Religious Worfhip, from Nature and Reafon. In two Books. By *David Martin*, late Paftor of the *French* Church at *Utrecht*. Tranflated from the *French*. The fecond Edition. 8*vo* 1725.

16 The Beauty of Holinefs in the Common-Prayer, as fet forth in four Sermons, preach'd at the *Rolls* Chapel in the Year 1716 The eighth Edition. To which is added, a *Rationale* on Cathedral Worfhip, or Choir Service. The fecond Edition. By *Thomas Biffe*, D. D. 8*vo*. 1721

17. Decency and Order in publick Worfhip, recommended in three Difcourfes preach'd in the Cathedral Church of *Hereford*. By *Thomas Biffe*, D D. Chancellor of the faid Church 8*vo* 1723.

18. Eight Sermons preach'd at the Cathedral Church of St. *Paul's* in Defence of the Divinity of our Lord Jefus Chrift, upon the Encouragement given by the Lady *Moyer*, and at the Appointment of the Lord Bifhop of *London*, &c. By *Daniel Waterland*, D. D. Mafter of *Magdalen* College in *Cambridge*. The fecond Edition. 8*vo*. 1720.

19. Dr. *Mangey*'s Practical Difcourfes upon the Lord's Prayer, preach'd before the Honourable Society of *Lincoln's-Inn*. The third Edition. 8*vo*. 1721.

20. A

BOOKS printed for W. and J. INNYS.

20. A Practical Discourse concerning the great Duty of Prayer. By *Richard Croſſinge*, B. D. Fellow of *Pembroke-Hall* in *Cambridge*. 8vo. 1720.

21. ——A Practical Discourse concerning the great Duty of Charity. 8vo. 1720.

22. The devout Soul, or Entertainment for a Penitent, consisting of Meditations, Poems, Hymns and Prayers, in two Parts. By *Tho. Coney*, D. D. Prebendary of *Wells*, and Rector of *Chedzey* in *Somerſetſhire*. 8vo. 1722.

23. Primitive Morality: or, the Spiritual Homilies of St. *Macarius* the *Egyptian*, full of very profitable Instructions concerning that Perfection which is expected from Christians, and which is their Duty to endeavour after. Done out of *Greek* into *Engliſh*, with several considerable Emendations, and some Enlargements from a *Bodleian* Manuscript, never before printed. 8vo. 1721.

24. Dr. *Lucas*'s Enquiry after Happiness. In three Parts. 1. Of the Possibility of obtaining Happiness. 2. Of the true Notion of human Life. 3. Of Religious Perfection. In two Vols. The fifth Edition. 8vo. 1717.

25. Twenty four *Sermons* preach'd on several Occasions. In two Vols. By *Richard Lucas*, D. D. The second Edition.

26. *Phyſico-Theology:* or, a Demonstration of the Being and Attributes of God from his Works of Creation, being the Substance of sixteen Sermons preach'd in St. *Mary-le-Bow* Church, *London*, at the Honourable Mr. *Boyle*'s Lectures, in the Years 1711 and 1712, with large Notes, and many curious Observations. By *W. Derham*, Canon of *Windſor*, Rector of *Upminſter* in *Eſſex*, and F. R. S. The sixth Edition. 8vo. 1723.

27. *Aſtro-Theology* · or, a Demonstration of the Being and Attributes of God, from a Survey of the Heavens. Illustrated with Copper Plates. The fifth Edition, 8vo. 1725.

28. A Defence of the Validity of the *Engliſh* Ordinations, and of the Succession of the Bishops in the Church of *England* · Together with Proofs, justifying the Facts advanced in this Treatise. Written in *French* by the Reverend Father, *Peter Francis Le Courayer*, Canon Regular and Librarian of St. *Genevieve* at *Paris*. To which is prefixed, a Letter of the Author to the Translator. 8vo. 1725.

29. A Discourse of Schism; shewing, I. What is meant by Schism. II. That Schism is a damnable Sin. III. That there is a Schism between the Establish'd Church of *England*, and the Dissenters. IV. That this Schism is to be charg'd on the Dissenter's Side. V. That the Modern Pretences of Toleration, Agreements in Fundamentals, *&c.*

4 will

will not excuse the Diffenters from being guilty of Schism. By *Thomas Bennet*, D D. Vicar of St. *Giles's Cripplegate*. The fourth Edition. 8*vo*. 1718.

30. The Indictment, Arraigment, Tryal and Judgment at large of tweny-nine Regicides, the Murtherers of his most Sacred Majesty King *Charles* the First, with their Speeches. 8*vo*. 1724.

31. *The Christian's Pattern:* or, A Treatife of the Imitation of Jefus Christ. By *Thomas a Kempis.* English'd by *George Stanhope*, D D. The tenth Edition 8*vo*. 1721.

32 A Version of the Pfalms of *David*, fitted to the Tunes read in Churches By Sir *John Denham*, Knight of the *Bath*. 8*vo*.

33 The Religious Philofopher or, the right Ufe of contemplating the Works of the Creator I. In the wonderful Structure of Animal Bodies, and in particular Man. II In the no lefs wonderful and wife Formation of the Elements, and their various Effects upon Animal and Vegetable Bodies And, III. In the moft amazing Structure of the Heavens, with all its Furniture. Defign'd for the Conviction of Atheifts and Infidels By that Learned Mathematician, Dr. *Nieuwentyt*. To which is prefix'd a Letter to the Tranflator, by the Reverend *J. T Defaguliers*, L. L. D. F R. S. The third Edition. Adorn'd with Cuts. 2 Vols. 4*to* 1724

34 The Religion of Nature delineated. The fourth Etion. 4*to* 1726.

35 An Analytick Treatife of Conick Sections, and their Ufe for refolving of Equations in determinate and indeterminate Problems. Being the Pofthumous Work of the Marquis *De L'Hofpital* 4*to*. 1723

36 A Commentary upon the Prophecy and Lamentations of *Jeremiah*. By *W. Lowth*, B D. 4*to*.

37. A Chronological Effay on the Ninth Chapter of the Book of *Daniel* · or, an Interpretation of the Prophecy of the feventy Weeks, whereby the *Jews*, in and for above 460 Years before our Saviour's Time, might certainly know the very Year in which the Meffias was to come. By *Peter Lancafter*, Vicar of *Bowden* in *Chefhire*, and fometime Student of *Chrift-Church* in *Oxford*. 4*to*. 1722.

Lately publifh'd for April 1726. (*being the* 16*th.*)

New Memoirs of Literature, containing an Account of new Books printed both at Home and Abroad, with Differtations upon feveral Subjects, mifcellaneous Obfervations, &*c*. N. B. Thefe Memoirs will be publifh'd every Month. Price 1 *s* each.

Lightning Source UK Ltd.
Milton Keynes UK
UKHW030803131219
355327UK00009B/996/P

9 781170 408872